La Haine (Hate)

(Mathieu Kassovitz, 1995)

Ginette Vincendeau

I.B. TAURIS
LONDON · NEW YORK

Published in 2005 by I.B. Tauris & Co. Ltd; reprinted 2009, 2010, 2011, 2012, 2014

6 Salem Road, London W2 4BU

175 Fifth Avenue, New York NY 10010

ibtauris.com

ISBN 1 84511 101 X

EAN 978 1 84511 101 4

A full CIP record for this book is available from the B

Typeset in Minion by Dexter Haven Associates Ltd, London

Printed and bound by CPI Group (UK) Ltd, Croydon, CR0 4YY

MIX

Paper from
responsible sources

FSC   FSC® C013604
www.fsc.org

Contents

Acknowledgements

First of all, I want to thank Philippa Brewster at I.B. Tauris for asking me to edit this new series of French Film Guides. *La Haine* is part of the first batch of publications, which also includes *Alphaville*, *Les Diaboliques* and *La Reine Margot*, in what I hope is the beginning of a long and fruitful series.

In the course of writing this book, as usual, many friends and colleagues have helped me with ideas, documentation, films and research assistance – among them José Arroyo, Tracey Bale, Chris Darke, Richard Dyer, Peter Graham, Susan Hayward, Stuart Henderson, Will Higbee, Elaine Lenton, Laurent Marie, Valerie Orpen, Richard Perkins, Julianne Pidduck, Clive Scott, Carrie Tarr and Leila Wimmer, to all of whom go my thanks. I especially want to thank Barbara Lehin and Min Lee for research assistance beyond the call of duty. I should also like to thank students on the national cinemas course at the University of Warwick, who with their enthusiasm and perceptive engagement with the film have also helped me clarify my thoughts. Last but not least, Simon Caulkin, as usual, provided invaluable support and brilliant editorial advice.

Note

Translations of quotes and other French material are my own, unless otherwise indicated.

Synopsis

La Haine opens with television footage of riots that took place the night before in the 'Cité des Muguets' housing estate (*cité*) on the outskirts of Paris, provoked by the brutal police assault on Abdel, a young *Beur* (person of second-generation North African origins), now in a coma. In the aftermath of the riot we discover damaged buildings and cars in the *cité*, and meet the film's three young protagonists: Saïd (Saïd Taghmaoui), a *Beur*, the Jewish Vinz (Vincent Cassel) and Hubert (Hubert Koundé), of black African origins. All three young men are unemployed. In the first half of the film we see them wander about, tell each other stories, meet friends and brothers, verbally assault television reporters, sisters, grandmothers and shopkeepers, visit the fence 'Darty' and, in Hubert's case, do a spot of drug dealing. Vinz reveals to his friends that he has picked up a gun lost by a policeman during

The three heroes of *La Haine* arrive in Paris; from left to right: Vinz (Vincent Cassel), Saïd (Saïd Taghmaoui) and Hubert (Hubert Koundé)

the riot; Saïd is impressed, Hubert horrified. They decide to visit Abdel in hospital but are turned away by the police, Abdel being in a critical condition. As they complain violently, Saïd is arrested and taken to the police station (itself wrecked in the riots), but is soon released thanks to Samir, a sympathetic local policeman. The three young men take the train to Paris.

In the city they first meet an old man in a café toilet who tells them an intriguing story about the Gulag. They then visit 'Astérix', a drug dealer who owes Saïd money, but the visit turns sour as Astérix and Vinz start a fight over guns. As they leave the apartment the three friends are stopped by the police (probably tipped off by the concierge), although Vinz manages to escape. While Saïd and Hubert are brutally humiliated by the police, Vinz attends a boxing match with friends from the estate. The three meet up again at Gare Saint-Lazare late at night, after missing the last train home. Back to wandering through Paris, they gatecrash an art gallery party but are thrown out for their disruptive behaviour. They attempt unsuccessfully to steal a car and learn through a giant television screen of Abdel's death. There is a violent confrontation with a group of skinheads; Vinz threatens to shoot the leader (Mathieu Kassovitz), but can't pull the trigger, despite Hubert's urging.

Back on the estate at dawn Vinz gives up his gun to Hubert. However, a police check turns to tragedy, and Vinz is accidentally shot by 'Notre Dame', a local policeman. Hubert walks back towards the group with Vinz's gun and threatens the policeman. The two are locked in a 'Mexican stand-off', with a gun at each other's head, while Saïd watches in horror. We hear a gunshot as the screen goes black.

Introduction

Mathieu Kassovitz's second feature film, *La Haine*, came out in France in May 1995 and internationally a few months later.[1] His first feature, *Métisse* (1993), had attracted some attention and prizes, but its public reception had remained modest. The impact of *La Haine*, on the other hand, was enormous, 'revealing' to the world both a topic – the Parisian *banlieue* (suburbs) – and a new film auteur.

The work of a relatively unknown 28-year-old director and with no star, this black and white chronicle of 24 hours in the life of a mixed-race young male trio from a run-down *banlieue* became hugely – and unexpectedly – successful, both commercially and critically. Among other things, Kassovitz was awarded the coveted Best Direction (*mise en scène*) prize at Cannes, and *La Haine* featured in the top 20 at the 1995 French box office. The film's high-profile release in the wake of Cannes was greeted by enthusiastic reviews, which hailed both the social contents and the energetic style of the film, as well as the charismatic central performances. There was also controversy: was Kassovitz exposing or exploiting his topic? As a middle-class white filmmaker, did he have the 'right' to speak about the *banlieue* and its multi-ethnic population? Furthermore, the coincidence between the contents of the film and real-life events, in particular riots in *banlieues* similar to that of the film that took place immediately after its release, sparked off huge debates about violence, the media and the *banlieue*, turning *La Haine* into a *phénomène de société* beyond its cinematic value.

Ten years on, of all the French films of the 1990s, *La Haine* is still one of the most widely screened and admired – and written about – nationally and internationally, and it has attained cult status, especially with younger generations. At the time of writing in 2004, for example, the Allociné.fr website still carries a lively discussion (clearly among young viewers) about the film, with some controversy but mostly ecstatic views such as 'the best French film of all times'.[2] The fact that both Kassovitz and lead actor Vincent Cassel have subsequently become major figures in French cinema has not harmed the reputation of the film either.

This book first of all provides an account of the various contexts within which the film was made, in terms of the film industry (the film's budget and material conditions and its production team) and French society (the *banlieue* and race relations), as well as the film genres in which the film may be inserted. There follows an in-depth analysis of the film itself, examining narrative structure, characterisation and style as well as issues of genre, gender and ideology. The book then explores the 'explosive' release of the film in France and abroad, as well as its national and international critical reception; this section surveys the wide amount of coverage in the press and tries to understand the surprising critical consensus that greeted the film – in order, by way of conclusion, to understand why, out of many other films about disaffected youth and problem suburbs, *La Haine* is the one that has caught the imagination. The final section of the book collects various appendices, including credits, filmography and bibliography, as well as a personal account of my visit to the place where the film was shot. Although all this material has been organised according to a classic chronological sequence, the reader is, of course, at liberty to jump straight to the analysis of the film in Chapter 2 – or, indeed, start with the reception and move back in time.

The aim of this book is both to document its making, structure, style and reception and to offer some interpretations. Mathieu Kassovitz is on record as having disliked some of the 'intellectual' discourse around his film.[3] But, whether he likes it or not, *La Haine* has entered our film culture and it deserves to be taken seriously, even as it gives great pleasure.

Notes

1   *La Haine* came out in November 1995 in the United Kingdom and February 1996 in the United States.
2   http://www.allociné.fr/film/critique_gen_cfilm=12551&affpress=0.html.
3   Charity, Tom, interview with Mathieu Kassovitz, *Time Out*, 15–22 November 1995, pp. 26–27.

1   Production contexts

I did not want a '*banlieue* film' made on a shoestring. I wanted the topic to be treated seriously.[1]

Mathieu Kassovitz

A young team

The director: Mathieu Kassovitz

Born on 3 August 1967 in Paris, Mathieu Kassovitz comes from a film background. His mother is the editor Chantal Rémy and his father the television director and occasional actor Peter Kassovitz, who played the shy young man in Jean-Luc Godard's *Vivre sa vie* in 1962. His films are mostly made for television, one important exception being *Jakob the Liar*, 1999, a Jewish ghetto story starring Robin Williams. It is clear that the family milieu fostered a cinephile atmosphere. As Kassovitz is fond of saying, 'My parents were in film. If they'd been bakers, I would've become a baker, but they were film-makers, so I became a film-maker.'[2] Young Mathieu was taken to see Stephen Spielberg's 1971 *Duel* by his father when he was ten, and at the age of 12 he was making short films in Super-8. As an adolescent he frequented Parisian art cinemas and film clubs, though his taste was for horror, science fiction and 'the fantastic',[3] and his references were Spielberg and Schwarzenegger rather than Fritz Lang or Renoir.[4] He read and produced fanzines about horror films. Nevertheless, he cites Georges Lucas' nostalgic *American Graffiti* (1973) – which he says he saw once a week for a whole year[5] – and especially Luc Besson's 1983 science fiction film *Le Dernier combat* as being particularly influential in determining his desire to make films. Besson's first feature showed Kassovitz that it was possible to make a genre film cheaply and to make films while still very young. He would in this respect emulate his model, since he was 25 when he made *Métisse* and 27 at the time of *La Haine*. The names of Spielberg and Lucas, to whom Martin Scorsese, Brian de Palma and Spike Lee would soon be added, as well as the taste for horror and science fiction (not normally French genres), spell out Kassovitz's love of American cinema. Although his Americanophilia seems to have been particularly acute (he went as far as to seek out the – then – only McDonald's restaurant in Paris after his weekly *American Graffiti* screenings), his tastes are typical of a generation of young men who came of age in the 1980s, when American cinema for the first time outstripped French cinema at the French box office. This was also the time when Kassovitz started taking an interest in hip-hop culture.

Kassovitz's family background left other important legacies. Peter Kassovitz comes from a Hungarian Jewish family. His own parents were both concentration camp survivors and he himself emigrated after the 1956 coup. Apart from an interest in this history, Mathieu Kassovitz has repeatedly celebrated the Jewish sense of humour he has inherited from his family, and in particular his paternal grandfather, who was a cartoonist; we will see how in *Métisse* and *La Haine* Jewishness plays an important part, although in these two films Kassovitz transposes its rituals, idiosyncrasies and jokes into a milieu decidedly more working class than his own. Kassovitz has also attributed his social conscience to the left leanings of his parents, whose filmographies bear witness to this.

Kassovitz left school around the age of 17, as he was already more attracted to the cinema, although he did not attend film school. Thus, unlike many of his contemporaries in the *jeune cinéma français* (young French cinema) trend, he is not an alumnus of the FEMIS,* which may go towards explaining his greater penchant for mainstream cinema, as we will discuss later. Thanks to his father Kassovitz frequented the studios, and he acknowledges the role of this connection[6] in helping him obtain his first trainee jobs. From these he graduated to second assistant director on a film by Paul Boujenah (*Moitié moitié*, 1989), and then first assistant director on industrial films; meanwhile, he began acting in a few movies, including some of his father's. With FF20,000 he had saved and a borrowed camera he finally made his first short in 1990 (at the age of 23), *Fierrot le pou*. The title is a pun on the personality of the film's hero, a geeky basketball player played by himself, and the title of Godard's *Pierrot le fou*, although Godard's

---

* FEMIS is the Ecole Nationale Supérieure des Métiers de l'Image et du Son.

relevance seems to stop there. This black and white film, which lasts seven minutes tells the simple story of a white basketball player who tries to impress a young black woman, but is quickly and comically upstaged by a more talented black player. Over the end credits, a rap song (by 'Rockin' Squat') can be heard, singing 'exploitation flows in the white man's veins'. The same year Kassovitz also directed *Peuples du monde*, a music video for French black rapper 'Tonton David'.

While working on *Fierrot le pou* Kassovitz had a crucial encounter with Christophe Rossignon, a young producer who would exert a significant influence on him. Rossignon helped Kassovitz finish *Fierrot le pou* and make another short, *Cauchemar blanc*, adapted from a famous strip cartoon by cult author 'Moebius' (Jean Giraud) about racism in the suburbs. The ten-minute black and white film shows four incompetent racist white men going on the rampage in a suburb one night, bent on attacking a North African man. Initially their attacks comically backfire: they crash their car into a telephone booth (which ends up on top of the car), one of them is knocked out, another pretends to be a policeman only to be arrested by a real (black) policeman. The silence and dignity of the North African contrast with the ludicrous rants of the whites – until we discover that this was all a dream, the 'nightmare' of the title. As the four men 'wake up', in the film's chilling

Mathieu Kassovitz, the director of *La Haine*, playing the male romantic lead in *Le Fabuleux destin d'Amélie Poulain*

coda off-screen, they beat and probably kill the North African, who is left lying on the ground.

At that point Kassovitz wanted to move on to making feature films, but Rossignon encouraged him to make a third short, *Assassins*, a story about violence that would act as a kind of pilot for his 1997 feature of the very similar name, *Assassin(s)*. The 1992 *Assassins*, at 11 minutes, is longer and more accomplished than the first two shorts and it is in colour. It shows two brothers who murder an old man in a suburban house. Apart from the helpless cries of the man, who is savagely beaten and tied to a radiator, the film focuses on the older brother teaching the younger one (played by Kassovitz) to overcome his panic in order to perform the killing – a concern with male 'education' into violence that will resurface in the 1997 feature. While *Cauchemar blanc* was awarded the Perspectives du Cinéma Award at the 1991 Cannes Film Festival, *Assassins* was more controversial, provoking the ire of Socialist Minister for Culture Jack Lang, who wrote to Kassovitz that the film was an 'incitement to murder'.[7] Lang's judgement may be over the top, but *Assassins'* sadistic focus on the old man's terror and the two killers' semi-comic behaviour does raise some uncomfortable issues – in particular, the kind of spectatorial engagement that is sought by the film in which fascination for violence is close to celebration, despite an evident desire to 'analyse'. For our purpose here, it is striking that the three shorts together condense the themes that are central to *La Haine*: the admiration for black men and hip-hop culture (*Fierrot le pou*), racism in the suburbs (*Cauchemar blanc*) and violence (*Assassins*). All three share a quasi-obsessive focus on troubled masculinity, which also prefigures *La Haine* and Kassovitz's subsequent films. Stylistically, apart from the use of black and white in two out of three, the shorts show Kassovitz's predilection for fluid long takes, which will reappear in *Métisse* as well as *La Haine*.

Kassovitz finally succeeded in making his first feature, *Métisse*, in 1993. In contrast to the male outlook of his shorts and, indeed, of *La Haine*, *Métisse* tells the story of Lola, a half-caste Catholic woman from the French West Indies (played by Julie Mauduech) who reveals to her two lovers, white Jewish Félix (Kassovitz) and black Muslim Jamal (Hubert Koundé), who until then are ignorant of each other's existence, that she is pregnant and that either of them could be the father. In interviews Kassovitz has cited as a source for *Métisse* his own interrogation about what he would feel if his girlfriend went out with a black man, an autobiographical angle reinforced by the fact that Mauduech was his partner at the time.[8] Beyond the autobiographical, as the title – which means half-caste – makes clear, the theme of race is central to *Métisse*, and the film again taps into French hip-hop culture with a theme rap song by 'Assassin' entitled 'La Peur du métissage' (fear of racial hybridity). The story is, however, treated in a lightly comic manner. The initially hostile rival male lovers end up best friends while looking after the heavily pregnant Lola. Although Félix is revealed by a test to be the biological father, both young men are united around the birth, which seems to solve all problems, in the tradition of French comedy (see Coline Serreau's 1985 *Trois hommes et un couffin* and Josiane Balasko's 1995 *Gazon maudit*, among others). The fact that Jamal is the son of a rich diplomat and a law student while Félix is a fast-food delivery man is refreshingly counter-stereotypical but, equally, serves to defuse serious issues around racism, given this atypical race/social hierarchy. Kassovitz comically indulges in blatant cinephilia, further emphasising the light aspects of the film: the plot echoes Spike Lee's *She's Gotta Have It* (1986), and the character he plays is an inept version of Lee's Mookie in his own *Do The Right Thing* (1989) – Kassovitz's outfit makes him look geeky (as in *Fierrot le pou*), and he endlessly falls off his bike and generally gets into trouble. Kassovitz's emulation of Spike Lee, but also his adolescent fixation on black hip-hop culture, are recognised by the film (at one point Jamal accuses Félix of 'playing at being the black man with [his] shitty rap music'), though not without self-indulgence.

With hindsight, what is also striking about *Métisse* is the degree of continuities with *La Haine*, notably in its cast. Hubert Koundé as Jamal anticipates Hubert (same actor, same wise persona) while Félix looks forward to Vinz and his Jewish family. Cassel, in a small role, plays Félix's brother, thus emphasising the overlap between Cassel and Kassovitz, whose real-life fathers additionally both appear in cameos in *Métisse*: Peter Kassovitz as a dull university lecturer, Jean-Pierre Cassel as Lola's gynaecologist. Félix's sister is called Sarah, like Vinz's sister in *La Haine*, and the same actress plays both characters.[9] Another casting bridge is provided by Rywka Wajsbrot (Félix's aunt in *Métisse* and Vinz's grandmother in *La Haine* – with, moreover, the same joke about green peppers) and Tadek Lokcinski, the actor who plays Félix's grandfather in *Métisse* and who turns out to be the man who tells the story in the toilets in *La Haine*. Finally, producer Rossignon plays a taxi driver in both films. A scene in which Félix and Jamal are arrested in the street and roughed up by the police anticipates a similar – though more violent – episode in *La Haine*. A thematic continuity between the two films is the absence in both narratives of parents and, especially, fathers, perhaps ironic in the light of the screen presence of both Kassovitz's and Cassel's real-life fathers. The young heroes represent a generation adrift. Finally, if *Métisse* is a more 'feminine' film than Kassovitz's other shorts and features, it fails to construct a proper subjectivity for Lola, quickly shifting to the two young men and the bond forming between them, foreseeing the masculine focus of *La Haine*.

Despite its charm and youthful zest, *Métisse* was not commercially successful, which Kassovitz attributes to an inadequate publicity campaign. It was shown in cinemas for only three weeks and sold 35,000 tickets in Paris and 85,000 in the rest of France, a poor score. On the other hand, the film attracted a certain amount of critical attention. Kassovitz was nominated for two Césars (for Best First Film and Most Promising Actor) in the 1994 ceremony, neither of which he got. He was, however, rewarded at the 1993 Paris Film Festival with a Special Jury prize and the Best Actor prize. Not bad for a film made on 16mm with a small crew, and without support from the CNC (Centre National de la Cinématographie).[10] For this reason, as Kassovitz proudly points out in several interviews, the end credits of *Métisse* bear the mention 'FTCNC' ('fuck the CNC') under the section 'Mathieu Kassovitz thanks...' Sincere as it may be, Kassovitz's combative attitude over *Métisse* and the CNC is also the first sign of his fraught relationship with the film establishment, including journalists and critics, which will be in evidence during the reception of *La Haine*, as discussed in Chapter 3, and even more so later, at the time of *Assassin(s)*.

In the period following the release of *Métisse*, Kassovitz's fortune rose in another direction: he was awarded the 1994 César for Best Actor and the 1995 Jean Gabin prize (awarded every year to a 'promising young actor') for his part in Jacques Audiard's successful thriller *Regarde les hommes tomber* (1994). In another display of attitude, he refused to collect his César, on the grounds that 'there is in French cinema a really rotten kind of code of good behaviour. [...] I am 27, I refuse to prostitute myself.'[11] Thus, if he was still relatively unknown as a director at the time of *La Haine*, he had begun to make a name for himself in critical circles and was on the rise as a promising if rebellious actor.

The production company

La Haine was produced by Les Productions Lazennec, a 'young' company founded by Alain Rocca in the late 1980s and noted first of all for its championing of short films, including Kassovitz's. Rocca has stated that, 'in order to discover Rochant, Vincent, Klapisch, Le Guay, Kassovitz, I went through festivals such as Clermont-Ferrand where short films dominate. It is the genre par excellence which enables you to discover real talents.'[12] Lazennec also quickly acquired a reputation for bankrolling young auteur films in touch with contemporary reality. As filmmaker Nicolas Boukhrief puts it, Rocca and Rossignon 'were *the* producers of the *jeune cinéma français*.'[13] Their roster of features preceding *La Haine* indeed contains several important small or medium-budget films that in different styles and genres brought new talents and new topics to French cinema – titles such as *Un monde sans pitié* (Eric Rochant, 1989), *Riens du tout* (Cédric Klapisch, 1992), *L'Odeur de la papaye verte* (Tran Anh Hung, 1993) and *Les Patriotes* (Eric Rochant, 1994). Journalist Alain Riou has argued in *Le Nouvel Observateur* that 'Lazennec was to [the 1990s] what *Cahiers du cinéma* was to the revolutionary filmmakers of the new wave'.[14] Riou's comparison is technically incorrect, since *Cahiers du cinéma* as a journal supported the new wave critically, not in terms of finance. A more accurate comparison would be with producers such as Georges de Beauregard and Anatole Dauman, who financially sustained the early new wave films. Nevertheless, the comparison with the new wave is pertinent insofar as Lazennec's support was also rooted in a deeply felt sympathy with the spirit of projects such as Kassovitz's shorts and early features. Even though *La Haine* turned out to be a bigger mainstream success than the other films, in its novelty, youthfulness and spot-on social relevance it was a typical 'Lazennec product' of the mid-1990s.

The Lazennec team included several producers, in particular Rocca, Adeline Lecallier and Rossignon. The latter, born in 1959 and thus in his mid-30s at the time of *La Haine*, joined Lazennec later than the first two producers. In what he describes as a 'fairy tale encounter' he met Kassovitz in his first week at Lazennec and immediately started working on the unfinished *Fierrot le pou*. The international success of the first film he produced (*L'Odeur de la papaye verte*) and then of *La Haine* quickly established him as an equal player in the company. As he said, 'I am no longer the youngest kid on the block. [...] Now Lazennec means Rocca, Lecallier, Rossignon.'[15] This was just reward for someone who had, according to his self-professed method, invested himself 'from A to Z' in supporting Kassovitz right from the start; he remained Kassovitz's producer through to *Assassin(s)*, after which the scale and style of Kassovitz's projects took him to more mainstream producers and then to Hollywood, though the two retained personal and professional ties (see Chapter 3).

The cast

Youth is also the hallmark of the film's cast, especially its central trio of actors, all of whom found their first proper starring role in *La Haine*. The lack of famous names can be seen as both aesthetically and financially determined. Established stars would obviously have been too expensive for a young director's film, although, as Vincent Cassel has pointed out, 'Mathieu could have got more money had he made the film with Isaac de Bankolé, Smaïn and Vincent Perez' (respectively, well-known black, *beur* and white actors).[16] Given their lack of previous exposure, it would be inappropriate to talk of a 'star persona' for these three young actors at the start of their career. I shall, therefore, discuss their looks and performance style in the analysis of the film in Chapter 2. Here I will briefly sketch out their backgrounds.

The fact that Vincent Cassel played Kassovitz's brother in *Métisse* is symbolic of the alter ego relationship developing professionally between the two, while they had been close friends for some time – a closeness acknowledged by Kassovitz, who had said: 'The only part I could play [in *La Haine*] was that of Vincent, and I preferred him to do it.'[17] Cassel (born in 1966) is virtually the same age as Kassovitz and like him a child of the film milieu. The son of respected actor Jean-Pierre Cassel (who appears among other well-known films in Jean Renoir's 1962 *Le Caporal épinglé* and in Jean-Pierre Melville's 1969 *L'Armée des ombres*), in 1995 Vincent Cassel had been 'in the business' for almost ten years. He had first trained for the circus and ballet, and then the theatre. Small film parts followed, until *La Haine* provided major recognition and led to other starring roles, and finally, as he put it, the chance to be more than 'the son of Jean-Pierre Cassel'.[18]

As if to compensate for the fact that both he and Cassel came from middle-class and artistic backgrounds, Kassovitz chose for his two other leads young actors who were sociologically closer to their characters. Hubert Koundé (Jamal in *Métisse*) comes from a family from Benin in West Africa, but was born in the Paris suburbs. In interviews in 1995 he was keen, however, to distance himself from the violent and deprived setting of *La Haine*: 'I live with my mother, my six brothers and my sister in a *cité* in the *banlieue* south of Paris, but it has nothing to do with the *cité* in *La Haine*. [...] We come from a modest background but we are not poor. I worked to pay for my studies just like my brothers did. Today I have a diploma in philosophy. I left university for the cinema when after *Métisse*, my first film, Mathieu Kassovitz offered me a big part in *La Haine*.'[19] The interviewer also points out rather patronisingly that, 'if in the film he speaks the slang of the suburbs, in front of me he speaks French like a professor of literature'. For his part, Saïd Taghmaoui, who met Kassovitz through Cassel, is closest of all three central actors to the part he plays, as a young *Beur* from the deprived '*cité des 3000*' in Aulnay-sous-bois, north-east of Paris.[20] Yet even he was not 'straight' from the *banlieue*. He had left school while very young and, after a vocational degree in catering, started acting in small parts in music videos, short films and finally Olivier Dahan's *Frères*. As he pointed out, journalists ignored this background and assumed 'I had been lifted straight from a *banlieue* and plonked into the film'.[21] Clearly, Kassovitz himself fell into this trap, to the question: 'Is he an actor?' answering: 'No, but he was a born actor! [...] No

Saïd (Saïd Taghmaoui)

Vinz (Vincent Cassel)

Hubert (Hubert Koundé)

need to create a character when you have him in front of you.'[22] Aside from their talent, the extraordinary 'rightness' of all three actors in their parts clearly stems from the fact that Kassovitz planned his film around them: 'When I started writing *La Haine*, I had these three in mind.'[23]

The rest of the cast, as we have seen, came in large part from *Métisse* and/or Kassovitz's immediate entourage, including *Métisse*'s heroine Julie Mauduech (who appears in a cameo in the art gallery), Kassovitz himself as the young skinhead roughed up by the three heroes, his father and Rossignon. Among other cameos, we should also mention Karin Viard as the other woman in the art gallery, Benoît Magimel as one of the boys hanging out in the *cité* (both of whom have since become major actors in their own right) and Vincent Lindon, the well-known actor who plays the drunk helping the three friends in their attempt to steal a car. Finally, one should note the presence of a significant number of *beur* actors in *La Haine*, such as Karim Belkhadra (Samir) and Zinedine Soualem (one of the plain-clothes policemen in Paris). Some small parts were played by members of the crew, for instance the beggar in the metro (costume designer Virginie Montel), and the film drew for its extras on inhabitants of Chanteloup-les-Vignes, where it was shot.

The project

Kassovitz says he started writing the script of *La Haine* on 6 April 1993, the day Makome M'Bowole, a young man from Zaïre (now the Democratic Republic of Congo), was shot while in police custody in a police station in the 18th arrondissement of Paris.[24] He wondered 'how a guy could get up in the morning and die the same evening, in this way'.[25] Makome's 'accidental' death was one of the many *bavures* (blunders or slip-ups) that have plagued the French police in recent decades. More than 300 mortal 'blunders' have been recorded since 1981 – common enough to become comic fare in such films as Claude Zidi's *Inspecteur La Bavure* (1980) and *Les Ripoux* (1984). For Kassovitz, however, they are no cause for mirth. Before Makome, another famous case, that of Malik Oussekine in 1986, had had particular resonance for him, and it is referred to in the opening montage of *La Haine*. The degree to which *La Haine* is 'about' police slip-ups is debatable, as we shall see, since, as the initial title for the project *Droit de cité* shows, the suburban environment is at least as important. Nevertheless, the unjust and often racist excesses of the police played an important part in the genesis and the structure of the film, which Kassovitz saw as countering *L.627*, Bertrand Tavernier's 1992 film about a Parisian police squad based on the memoirs of a former policeman: 'I wanted to show the opposite vision, that of the young of the *cités*.'[26]

Tadek Lokcinski (man in toilets)

Christophe Rossignon (producer/taxi driver)

Karin Viard (left), Julie Mauduech (centre), with Hubert Koundé

Peter Kassovitz (right) as gallery owner

Mathieu Kassovitz as skinhead

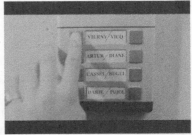

Names of crew and cast on Astérix's letter box

As we saw above, the cast of *La Haine* was already part assembled from *Métisse*. From the technical crew Kassovitz retained several members and in particular the director of photography, Pierre Aïm (who would also shoot *Assassin(s)*). At some FF15,000,000 ($28,000,000), *La Haine* was a medium-budget production. It was cheap in comparison to other major French successes of that year, across genres; for instance the drama *Elisa* (FF73,000,000), the fantasy film *La Cité des enfants perdus* (FF97,000,000), the comedy *Les Anges gardiens* (FF142,000,000) and the heritage film *Le Hussard sur le toit* (FF176,000,000 – at the time the most expensive French film ever).[27] On the other hand, *La Haine* was relatively expensive for a film by a young auteur: as a point of comparison, Jean-François Richet's *État des lieux*, another gritty black and white film about the *banlieue*, which also came out in 1995, cost FF150,000 (100 times less). As Kassovitz said, 'We could have done [*La Haine*] for FF300,000 but it would have been a different film. I did not want a "*banlieue* film" made on a shoestring. I wanted the topic to be treated seriously, the spectator to realise they were not being simply presented with guys who put their caps on the wrong way and said "yo". It is a sophisticated work of fiction, not a documentary on the life of the *cités*.'[28] Kassovitz applied for the *avance sur recettes* but failed to get it, partly as the result of the attitude evoked above: he (and Rossignon) declined the opportunity to submit a rewrite of the script.[29] Instead, the film gathered its budget in the now classic French way, with contributions from television channels, in this case Le Studio Canal+ and La Sept, and with participation from investment companies (Soficas), though it was by no means easy, as at the time neither Rossignon nor Kassovitz was known.[30] Last-minute problems with distributors meant that Kassovitz had to waive his fee,[31] and, according to Rossignon, the financial success of *La Haine* benefited Le Studio Canal+ rather than Lazennec.[32]

Contrary to common assertion, *La Haine* was not shot in black and white; it was shot in colour and then printed in black and white (a colour project was thought to have better chances of attracting the needed investment). The plan was to transfer to black and white for the release, although Rossignon and Kassovitz at one point envisaged re-releasing the film on television in colour if the black and white version was unsuccessful.[33] For aesthetic reasons Kassovitz also considered at one point showing the *cité* part of the film in black and white and the Paris sequences in colour, or the *cité* in 16mm and Paris in 35mm, but rejected this as 'too dogmatic'.[34] In the end, of course the entire film remained in black and white, with only one brief moment towards the beginning in colour, an image of the earth going up in flames. Subsequently, even this (in colour on the VHS versions of the film) has been transferred to black and white, as Kassovitz now considers the insertion of colour 'hackneyed'.[35]

La Haine was shot between September and November 1994 on location in the La Noë *cité* in Chanteloup-les-Vignes on the far north-western edge of Paris, as well as in Paris itself, for example in the Gare Saint-Lazare and the shopping mall of Les Halles. The choice of Chanteloup-les-Vignes is interesting. Kassovitz has repeatedly stated that he did not want 'a derelict *cité* of the kind they exhibit in the media, but a more ordinary one, in order to show that their explosive problems are not caused by architecture'.[36] If he is right on the last point, La Noë in Chanteloup-les-Vignes is hardly an 'ordinary' *cité*, as discussed later on. Kassovitz took the job of filming this – new to him – environment seriously. His choice was partly aesthetically driven and largely necessity: 12 towns were apparently contacted and only Chanteloup-les-Vignes accepted, as long as there was no publicity about the shooting, either beforehand, during or afterwards[37] (this promise was not entirely fulfilled, as some photographs and articles attest – see Chapter 3). As he said, 'We went to the *cité* three months before shooting started [accounts vary: in some interviews he says two months]. The actors and I lived there in a three-bedroom flat in order to have a minimum of credibility in our own eyes',[38] and to show that 'we were not shooting *Navarro* [a popular French television crime series]'.[39] The decision to become acquainted with the local inhabitants seems to have been fruitful and Kassovitz reports integrating some features, such as the fact that the children of La Noë knew the local cops by their first names, into the script.[40] At the same time, all was not plain sailing; some inhabitants were uncooperative, and Kassovitz was reticent about the problems: 'Some of them refused to have any contact with us. Naturally we had some problems, but I don't want to talk about it.'[41] In a later interview he was a little more forthcoming: 'We slept there, we spoke to the blokes from the *cité*. Things went well during shooting, even though the situation was always "on the edge". Stones were thrown at us, but it was just kids playing.'[42] He perceptively summed up the root of the problem: 'We were there for two months, they were there for life.'[43] There is no reason to doubt that he and his production team were in good faith, but the gap was ultimately unbridgeable – something that would return to haunt them after the film's release (see Chapter 3).

Despite these difficulties, Kassovitz has described the experience as 'a powerful shoot', and his relationship with the crew as 'brilliant'.[44] In any case, shooting was economical. Important action scenes (such as the imaginary shooting of the traffic wardens) were prepared on a storyboard[45] and Kassovitz says he shot 'no more than four takes per shot', ending up with about ten hours of usable rushes, which were edited digitally. Ten days later, he had a rough cut of 110 minutes.[46] Two scenes were deleted (one of a fight with the police after the *cité* rooftop scene, and one in which Vinz looks at a man sleeping rough on the pavement in Paris), both of which can be seen on the Canal+ DVD, and a few episodes were tightened (such as the switching off of the Eiffel Tower). Further technical details are discussed in Chapter 2 with the analysis of the film. For the moment I will turn to the most important social context for the film, that of the *banlieue*.

The Parisian *banlieue* and its images

The fact that *La Haine* is set in a deprived *banlieue* and that the main characters are *banlieusards* is absolutely central to the identity of the film, despite the fact that half of the film actually takes place in central Paris. In this respect, *La Haine* contributed another important piece of 'evidence' to an already huge dossier in the sociology of contemporary France – adding to a plethora of books and articles, conferences, press reports, television programmes, films and internet websites. It is impossible to do justice to such a massive debate here, but before moving on to an analysis of the film I will sketch out the main lines of this sensitive sociological issue – taking Chanteloup-les-Vignes, where the film was shot, as a case study – and of the cinematic 'genre' that the film may (or may not) have given birth to.

Banlieues, cités *and the* fracture sociale

In the proverbial phrase, *La Haine* was in the right place at the right time. The film, which begins with images of riots and ends on a fatal shoot-out, recalled real-life riots that spread through the suburbs of Paris and other large French cities (Lyon, Marseille, Lille) through 1990–1992, when, following riots in Vaulx-en-Velin (near Lyon), a 'tidal wave' of unrest spread to places like Sartrouville, Mantes-la-Jolie and Val Fourré.[47] The film also uncannily foreshadowed others, notably in 1995 and 1997, including in Chanteloup-les-Vignes. Despite Kassovitz's insistence that *La Haine* was fictional, his film thus acquired a semi-documentary status, and a debate raged about the film's 'responsibility' in the later riots (discussed in Chapter 3).

Released on 31 May, *La Haine* also happened to come out shortly after the right-wing Jacques Chirac was elected President of the Republic on 7 May 1995, defeating the Socialist François Mitterrand, whose portraits can be seen on the walls of the police stations in the film, since it was shot in late 1994. Chirac's electoral campaign was dominated by themes of exclusion and '*fracture sociale*' (social divide),[48] outlining a 'global politics against exclusion' that targeted the estimated six million French people living below the poverty line and their worsening social exclusion – young people in the deprived *cités*, such as the three heroes of *La Haine* being a particular target.

At this point a word about the term *banlieue* is necessary. As many English-speaking writers observed when *La Haine* came out, 'suburbs' have specific connotations in France. In the United Kingdom and the United States deprived enclaves tend to be located in inner cities, while 'suburbs' connote a comfortable, middle-class environment. For this reason, I will tend to use the word *banlieue* rather than suburb. Similarly, I will retain the French word *cité* to designate the kind of housing in which the first half of the film takes place, as the British word 'estate' can have different meanings and the American term 'projects' refers too narrowly to the US context. The word *banlieue* initially designated a band of territory (of one *lieue* – about four kilometres – wide) that came under the legal jurisdiction (*ban*) of a city.[49] Although all large cities have a *banlieue,* my discussion will mostly refer to the Paris outskirts, given the film's location.

Of all major capitals, Paris developed in a uniquely circumscribed way. Since the 12th century a series of concentric ramparts have surrounded the city, which in turn incorporated the immediate areas outside (*faubourgs*), until the city's present shape was arrived at in the mid-19th century, when the fortifications created a no man's land immediately outside, a *zone* between the city and the expanding *banlieues*. This space, in which first gardens and then *bidonvilles* (shanty towns) flourished, was filled with 1930s social housing. It now also houses the *périphérique* motorway. More than in other capital cities, there is thus a sharp disjunction between the city of Paris and its surrounding *banlieue* outside.

Until the Second World War the Parisian *banlieue* evoked a semi-rural environment of small houses with gardens. This changed sharply in the post-war period. The economic boom and rapid expansion of Paris during the 'trente glorieuses' (1945–1975), especially under President Charles De Gaulle (1958–1969), demanded a massive building programme to house both immigrants and French workers, who flocked to the city from the land. The architects of the 1960s went for concrete gigantism in the building of the so-called *grands ensembles*, evidence of what Keith Reader calls 'cut-price modernist vision',[50] betrayed by the names of the most notorious *cités*: *Les 4,000* in La Courneuve, *Les 3,000* in Aulnay-sous-bois, not to mention the 12,000 flats of the most famous *grand ensemble*, Sarcelles. At that point in the 1960s the *banlieue* began to acquire its narrow sense and sinister image of bad housing and social deprivation, despite the fact that there are middle-class *banlieues*, especially to the west of the city, and that the working-class *banlieues* themselves are far from being uniform in population or architecture.

The industrial housing of the *grands ensembles*, for a long time predominantly referred to as HLM (habitation à loyer modéré – i.e. council housing), was built in high-rise tower blocks (*tours*) and long 'walls' (*barres*), filled with grids of identical flats nicknamed 'rabbit hutches' (*cages à lapins*). Although the HLMs were social housing that, with hot water and central heating, constituted progress, their disadvantages quickly became apparent: paper-thin walls, permanently broken-down lifts, damp cellars; few shops and cafés, and a lack of cultural venues. In a bitter joke, Jean-Luc Godard in *Alphaville* (1965) has Lemmy Caution (Eddie Constantine) call an HLM 'hôpital de longue maladie' (hospital for long illness). In the 1970s the pop singer Renaud sang: 'Il est pourri [rotten] mon HLM.' Solutions were sought. Some of the gigantic blocks were demolished. Better housing was built, with smaller blocks and vernacular designs. But the need for suitable building land pushed further out of the metropolis, and social problems worsened. The term *cité* replaced HLM as the symbol of so-called 'difficult', 'sensitive' or even 'hot' areas. This is true of La Noë in Chanteloup-les-Vignes which contrary to Kassovitz's claim for its 'ordinariness', was almost from the start considered by experts 'a test-town, an observatory of urban difficulties'.[51]

La Noë was built in 1972 near the village of Chanteloup-les-Vignes, 30 kilometres from central Paris. Its architect, Emile Aillaud (President Georges Pompidou's official architect), designed it in a new style meant to counter the modernist excesses evoked above. La Noë is composed of small, curved buildings, as opposed to the brutal linearity of the earlier *grands ensembles*. Only ten years after it was built, however, wear and tear was already serious. In 1982 buildings were upgraded and roof gables, pillars and decorative balconies added. This did not stop La Noë from developing acute problems, although, as Hervé Vieillard-Baron argues, 'despite many technical errors, the buildings were quite correct and the urban space agreeable. Architecture does not explain everything. [...] A *cité* that had been conceived "poetically" by its architect rapidly turned into a "social dustbin"',[52] and a town that according to its mayor, Pierre Cardo, had the biggest municipal deficit in France.[53] This was the result of demographic policies that amounted to social apartheid, combined with acute economic problems.

La Noë was initially built to house the workers of the Chrysler (later Talbot) car factory in nearby Poissy. The company systematically exploited unskilled immigrant workers (often recruiting them directly in North Africa) at lower than average salaries. The automation of the factory in 1980–1984 and a crisis in the motor industry in general produced chronic unemployment in Chanteloup-les-Vignes. This was compounded by the systematic allocation of 'problem' French families and a higher than average proportion of immigrant families to the *cité*; the population by the late 1980s was 70% non-metropolitan French. In addition, the *cité* included a higher than average number of children, who then swelled the proportion of unemployed in the mid-1990s. Vieillard-Baron also points to a planning fault common to many *cités*: La Noë suddenly and dramatically increased the population of Chanteloup-les-Vignes (from 2,000 to 10,000 within a few years); it was built some distance from the village, and 'the gap between hill for old village and flood plain for the new *cité* produced a reject phenomenon [...] The people from the high "village" ignored the "nomads" from down below.'[54] Symbolising this, there was no direct access between the village and *cité*, whose only opening was towards the immense, empty landscape of fields on the other side; it took three years to build the railway station, which was set on fire on the day of its inauguration. For Vieillard-Baron, such a combination of factors, together with bad management, accentuated the deplorable image of La Noë and accelerated its slide towards becoming a 'ghetto' with endemic deprivation and racism.[55] (For a personal view of La Noë, see Appendix 3.)

Not all *banlieues* combine all these factors. As Vieillard-Baron puts it: 'The 18m inhabitants in French *banlieues* are not all destined to live a nightmare.'[56] Yet La Noë reflects a widespread crisis, which a series of urban improvement policies tried to tackle. In 1991 a short-lived Ministry for the City was created, though this provoked mostly anger and derision.[57] More recently, a government department for 'integration and struggle against exclusion' has been set up. On 26 October 1995, after more violent riots, Jacques Chirac announced, on French television, a plan for 'national urban integration' meant to lead to a 'Marshall plan for the *banlieue*'.

Unfortunately, since the time of *La Haine*, the situation both in Chanteloup-les-Vignes and in other 'sensitive' *banlieues* has not improved. In January 2000 the daily *Libération* reported that 'fights between adolescents and policemen are frequent and violent in Chanteloup-les-Vignes'.[58] 'Gangs of young men impose their violent law on a terrorised and abandoned majority',[59] and fight with other gangs for their territory – for instance, in January 2001 rival gangs from Chanteloup-les-Vignes and Mantes-la-Jolie fought each other at La Défense. Security and anti-racist measures have now risen to the top of the agenda for the Chirac administration. The revived 'Marshall plan for the *banlieue*' includes measures aimed at improving 'social hybridity' and tax rebates to attract business to the suburbs, the latter supported by Pierre Cardo, the forceful mayor of Chanteloup-les-Vignes.[60] It is uncertain whether these measures will be more successful than earlier ones.

Is there a film de banlieue?

When *La Haine* came out, *Cahiers du cinéma*, alongside its review of the film, ran an article entitled 'Is there a *banlieue-film*?'. It thus confirmed the status of Kassovitz's film as epitome of a new 'genre', despite the fact that representations of the *banlieue* in French cinema were hardly new. However, the high visibility of *La Haine* and the fact that, in 1995 alone, at least four other films – *Raï* (Thomas Gilou), *Douce France* (Malik Chibane), *État des lieux* (Jean-François Richet) and *Bye Bye* (Karim Dridi) – qualified for the label attracted attention. Did these films constitute a 'genre'? And, if so, how does *La Haine* fit into it?

Until the 1960s the *banlieue* was represented as an idyllic location, offering relief from the noisy city, in populist films such as Marcel Carné's *Nogent, Eldorado du dimanche* (1929), Julien Duvivier's *La Belle équipe* (1936) and Denys de la Patellière's *Rue des prairies* (1959), or semi-rural spaces as in Carné's *Le Jour se lève* (1939). Alternatively, documentaries portrayed them as places of archaic or even 'poetic' poverty, for instance Georges Lacombe's *La Zone* (1928) and Eli Lotar's *Aubervilliers* (1945). From the 1960s representations changed dramatically, echoing the shifts in population and architecture evoked above. Documentaries recorded the old *banlieues* and the building of the new ones, among them Maurice Pialat's *L'Amour existe* (1960) and Chris Marker's *Le Joli mai* (1962). However, I shall here concentrate on fictional representations. The films in question cut across different genres, and French scholars have attempted to classify them in various ways.[61] While making reference to some of this work, I identify two major trends, which I call 'aesthetic' and 'sociological', though, inevitably, some films share both tendencies. The aesthetic tendency includes films such as Jacques Tati's *Mon oncle* (1958), Jean-Luc Godard's *Une femme mariée* (1964), *Deux ou trois choses que je sais d'elle* (1966) and *Numéro deux* (1975), Marguerite Duras' *Le Camion* (1977), Eric Rohmer's *Les Nuits de la pleine lune* (1984), *L'Ami de mon amie* (1987) and *Conte d'hiver* (1992), Alain Corneau's *Série noire* (1979), Claire Simon's *Scènes de ménage* (1991) and Jean-Claude Brisseau's *De bruit et de fureur* (1987), Bertrand Blier's *Les Valseuses* (1973), *Buffet froid* (1979), *Trop belle pour toi* (1989) and *Un deux trois soleil* (1993). In these predominantly auteur films, the *banlieue* exists as an index of modernity, seen positively or negatively depending on the point of view of the director, as well as the type of *banlieue* portrayed. Thus, Godard's films are highly critical of the *grands ensembles*, Duras highlights the emptiness of the landscape, while on the other hand Rohmer views the new middle-class suburbs positively. In all these films, however, the *banlieue* primarily serves as background to other concerns, such as an analysis of

Three views of the *cité* of La Noë in Chanteloup-les-Vignes as seen in *La Haine*

consumer society, existential despair, new lifestyles or sexual politics. As José Baldizzone says of Blier's films: 'The director chooses these places [the *banlieue*] not so much to depict them as to reveal a profound dysfunction in society.'[62] As is often the case in French auteur cinema, the desire to avoid the derogatory label of 'sociological film' is manifest in the foregrounding of an innovative, distancing aesthetic agenda: Tati's comic techniques in *Mon oncle*, the dichotomy between sound and image in *Deux ou trois choses* or *Le Camion*, the split screen in *Numéro deux*, the extravagance of Blier's films, the 'excess' of language in Rohmer's films, the hallucinatory apparitions in *De bruit et de fureur*.

On the 'sociological' side are films where the *banlieue* is more centrally a topic as well as a decor and where the stylistic approach is more naturalistic, although as for the auteur films there is huge variety: Pierre Granier-Deferre's *Le Chat* (1971), Gérard Pirès' *Elle court, elle court la banlieue* (1973), Maurice Pialat's *Loulou* (1979), René Allio's *Rude journée pour la reine* (1983), Serge Le Péron's *Laisse béton* (1984), Coline Serreau's *Romuald et Juliette* (1989) and *La Crise* (1992), Gérard Lauzier's *Le Plus beau métier du monde* (1996) would not be bracketed together if it was not for their *banlieue* setting. This 'sociological' category includes a range of film genres, from naturalist drama (*Loulou*) to comedy. In the latter, the *banlieue* is frequently used to provide contrast with plush Parisian surroundings (*Romuald et Juliette*), or to satirise living difficulties such as transport (*Elle court, elle court la banlieue*). Films such as *Le Chat*, the prologue of Henri Verneuil's *Mélodie en sous-sol* (1963) and *Rude journée pour la reine* pointedly record the contrast between two types of *banlieue* – the old (individual housing) and the new (high-rise blocks) – and evoke a visual space that cuts across all tendencies, where the *banlieue* is a borderline, heterogeneous space that is neither town nor country, and in some cases deserves to be called a no man's land.

Within this highly varied corpus a 'sub-genre' within the sociological tendency arose in the 1980s, consisting of films that conspicuously narrow the *banlieue* down to the *cités*, with their brutal architecture, multi-ethnic population and social problems. These are the *banlieue-films* evoked by Thierry Jousse and several other writers at the time of *La Haine*, a category that includes, prominently, *beur* films such as Mehdi Charef's *Le Thé au harem d'Archimède* (1985), Malik Chibane's *Hexagone* (1994) and *Douce France* (1995), Thomas Gilou's *Raï* (1995) and Olivier Dahan's *Frères* (1994) and Richet's *État des lieux* (1995) and *Ma 6-T va crack-er* (1997). These films present the originality of being frequently made by people originating *from* the *banlieue*. They create a recognisable – not to say limited – visual iconography that makes sense largely in opposition to the dominant urban iconography in French cinema, that of Paris. Although this is a feature of all the *banlieue* films evoked above, which always show or suggest the nearby big city, in the *'banlieue-films'* of the 1980s and 1990, the contrast is more marked. Ugly blocks of flats, often covered in obscene graffiti, contrast with beautiful apartments; encounters take place in run-down staircases, rooftops or cellars as opposed to bustling cafés and restaurants; empty car parks and desolate open spaces with burnt grass replace elegant boulevards, parks and picturesque streets. To the animated modernity, culture and romanticism of Paris is substituted a space of isolation, apathy, deprivation and fear. Many of the films stage visits to Paris, largely to make the contrast between city and *banlieue* more tangible; these episodes frequently include symbolic scenes of exclusion, from a club, a shop, the métro, etc., as in *La Haine*. Finally, as well as reducing the concrete environment of the *banlieue* to the *cité*, these films frequently boil down their inhabitants to groups of young men. As we will see, in all these respects *La Haine* is no exception. This shared iconography does not cancel out the diversity of the films – for example, the politicised *État des lieux* is far from the more consensual *Hexagone*. Rather than a genre, one can at best refer to a cycle or a series of films linked by a location.

In this spectrum, contrary to René Prédal, who sees it as 'unclassifiable',[63] I believe *La Haine* occupies a unique bridging position. From the 'sociological' trend, it takes a genuine interest in the deprived *banlieue* as setting and topic, as well as in its inhabitants. However, in contrast to the naturalism of most of these films, it has recourse to the stylistic distanciation of the 'aesthetic' films. Yet this is not the avant-garde distanciation of a Godard or a Brisseau, or the strangeness of a Blier. Kassovitz's ability to structure his film along classical lines, rework elements of American culture and deploy an exhilarating style, while respecting the 'local colour' of the *cité*, explain its extraordinary success. Ironically, whereas many *films de banlieue* and *beur* films emerge genuinely from within the *cités*, they have remained home products, whereas the more culturally hybrid *La Haine*, made by a team largely from outside the *cités*, has succeeded in exporting the 'feel' of this territory.

Other images: same clichés?

I have spent some time delineating the context of the *banlieue-films* because *La Haine* has been repeatedly seen against this background in critical discourse. Yet, for the majority audience seeing *La Haine* in France, especially young viewers, the main point of reference would have been television, not auteur films. And, as it turns out, despite the dominant critical discourse that sees *La Haine* in total opposition to television images, the latter are particularly relevant to it for other reasons too.

Marie-Claude Taranger's illuminating study of the spread of television programmes about the *banlieue* over the period 1989–1993 presents a series of self-reinforcing images, characters and situations, so persistent that she labels it a 'genre', similar to the western in terms of unity of iconography and action.[64] From a large spread of broadcasts on the main terrestrial channels, encompassing evening news, chat shows, reportage, documentaries and magazines, she isolates the following recurrent elements: *decor* (tower blocks, concrete buildings, graffiti, the proximity of a big city); *main characters* (groups of young men, immigrants and 'native', policemen); *action* (drama hingeing around a crisis, typically a theft or the death/injuring of a young 'immigrant' at the hands of the police, followed by an 'explosion of violence', clashes with the police, cars set ablaze); *themes* (drugs, unemployment, violence); *point of view* (a distant gaze: 'the *banlieue* is another world which you visit like a foreign country';[65] it even has its own language, *verlan*). Across all programmes, a catastrophic picture is endlessly repeated. Taranger contrasts this predictable scenario with other sources of information, such as sociological studies (and a few atypical programmes), which reveal a huge variety of decors, events, characters and points of view. She concludes that 'it is clear that the nature of the enquiry determines the images obtained. [...] Such an exploration can only deliver what it is designed to find.'[66] In her opinion, this hegemonic televisual discourse serves a conservative ideology designed to maintain an image of the *banlieue*, especially its 'immigrants', as violent and dangerous. Indeed, as the Communist daily *L'Humanité* has ironically commented, these images are avidly 'sought by channels like TF1 [the largest privatised television channel], which draw from them an ideal decor, sensationalism, blood, morality'.[67]

Beyond political debate, the potential influence of these images on people from the *banlieue* has been noted. In the words of journalist Natacha Wolinski, these images frequently 'devalue even more what is already devalued', making 'the *cité des 4,000* look like Sarajevo'. Wolinski quotes Boris Seguin, an expert on *banlieue* culture: 'Young people have integrated a mythology of the *banlieue*. Sometimes you don't know if they are really speaking of their *cité* or if they speak from pre-existing representations which they find in the media.'[68] Georges Ferreboeuf, press officer for a 'difficult' *banlieue*, puts it like this: 'Parisians come here with ready-made clichés and a partial view in mind. They show reality within a narrow framework, neglecting the "off-screen": everyday life.'[69] This is not just PR rhetoric. From François Maspéro and Anaïk Frantz's ethnographic journey through the suburbs, *Les Passagers du Roissy-Express*,[70] to Bertrand and Niels Tavernier after their experience of filming *De l'autre côté du périphérique* (1997), many have voiced concern at the gap between the multi-layered reality of the *banlieue* and its dominant representation through violent young males, only to be countered with the – circular – justification that it is violence that grabs the headlines. This latter phenomenon is illustrated by Didier Daeninckx's brilliantly ironic short story 'Rodéo d'or',[71] based on real events, in which television journalists pay hooligans to joyride for their cameras, with tragic consequences.

So where does this leave *La Haine*? It will be obvious that the film's set of events is uncannily similar to the 'predictable scenario' of television coverage. Thus, contrary to the dominant critical discourse about the film (see Chapter 3), *La Haine* cannot be said to 'reveal' the *banlieue* to its French audience; nor, more fundamentally, does it counter the hegemonic television discourse. On the contrary it recycles – in a radically different cinematic style – a deeply ingrained, dominant set of images. It is interesting in this respect that on the documentary about the making of the film, as the three leads are interviewed in their Chanteloup-les-Vignes flat, it is the middle-class Cassel who says 'the *banlieue* is shit', while Taghmaoui and Koundé, both *banlieusards*, remain silent.[72] The interesting question is why it should have been perceived as so new and different – a point that I hope to elucidate in this book.

At the same time as it shares the reductive view of the *banlieue* in its focus on the catastrophic scenario of youthful male violence, *La Haine* explicitly reflects on it in a way that is both sophisticated and entertaining. Yet Taranger argues that the pernicious force of the hegemonic television images of the *banlieue* is also that they remain in place even 'when journalists or films seem to depart from this common opinion or even explicitly profess other views'.[73] Another key question about *La Haine* in this respect will therefore be whether the film manages, through its overt critique of 'the media', to break the cycle of self-reinforcing discourse or not.

Banlieue-*speak and* verlan

The focus on youth in media representations of the *banlieue*, including *La Haine*, entails certain images, but also sounds: a recognisable accent and the slang form known as *verlan*. While this has become one of the clichés about the *banlieue* (as Taranger argues), it nevertheless contributes to the social reality of this social environment. *Verlan* is an ancient form of back-slang revived in the 1970s, in which syllables are inverted: *té-ci* instead of *ci-té* for example. The pop singer Renaud's 1975 hit 'Laisse béton' (*béton* is an inversion of *tomber*, to fall – *laisse tomber/laisse béton* meaning 'drop it') was a landmark in the spread of *verlan*, which further entered the culture through films with titles such as Claude Zidi's 1984 *Les Ripoux* (*verlan* for *pourri*, corrupt) and Josiane Balasko's 1987 *Les Keufs* (*verlan* for *flic*, cop). Other words have entered the national vocabulary, such as *meuf* (femme, woman) and, of course, *beur* (*arabe*); in fact, *beur* is so common that a further form of *verlan* has transformed it, in turn, into *rebeu*. Yet *beur*, while being possibly the most universally understood *verlan* term, is also the most problematic. Like 'black' in the United States, '*beur*' was claimed with pride by the *Beurs* in the 1980s. Two decades later it is rejected by a growing number of people of Maghrebi origins. For instance, the filmmaker Karim Dridi, who was born in Tunisia, sees it as 'invented by the Socialists at the beginning of the 1980s'.[74] He points out that, on the one hand, not all '*Beurs*' are Arabs, and on the other hand, that many '*Beurs*' are French. Thus, the term simultaneously increases the 'otherness' of those it designates and erases differences, within them.

Like all forms of slang, *verlan* is thus a marker of identity, however controversially. It designates a group, a clan, stressing its cohesion against the outside world. In its contemporary use, *verlan* is not specifically the language of criminals (unlike original *argot*), yet its association with the *cités* has given it an illicit connotation, contributing to the perception of the *banlieue* as 'dangerous' and 'other'. Like other kinds of slang, it also possesses a playful dimension,[75] one in evidence in the film. The list of *verlan* words in the dialogue of *La Haine* is, however, restricted to fairly common words in order not to alienate viewers. Subtitles were rejected as patronising and unnecessary, and a few passages re-recorded for purposes of clarity. The humour and flavour of *verlan* will unavoidably be lost to non-French speakers, who have to rely on the English subtitles (which, moreover, use very marked American slang). For those unfamiliar with *verlan*, a list of the main expressions used in the film is available in a glossary in Appendix 5.

The linguistic specificity of *La Haine* is not restricted to the presence of *verlan* in the dialogue. It is the *degree* to which the characters use it, their accents and the way they mix French/*verlan* with other linguistic imports and neologisms that designates their language as *banlieue*-speak. The recurrent insults of 'bâtard' (bastard) and 'nique ta mère' (literally 'fuck your mother' or 'motherfucker') mix North African slang ('nique') with American imports. A set of French neologisms has also appeared over the last 10–20 years, with expressions such as 'trop' (too much) added in front of many words (like 'so' in English) and expressions such as 'avoir la haine' meaning 'to hate', where standard French would use the verb 'haïr' or 'détester'. Thus, the very title of the film, which derives from 'avoir la haine', signals *banlieue*-speak. There is a declamatory, raucous musical quality to the intonation of young *banlieue* inhabitants, which distinguishes them sharply from their parents' generation, across racial differences – a kind of speaking particularly well illustrated by Saïd Taghmaoui in the film. This (to a French ear) highly recognisable intonation, combined with *verlan* and American/North African imports, forms a patois with aggressively macho, sexual connotations, similar to the lyrics of rap songs. While *banlieue*-speak has been seen by some sociologists as an expression of subcultural creativity, there are dissenting voices. In particular, *beur* writer Azouz Begag, talking of a '*fracture linguistique*' parallel to the '*fracture sociale*', argues that it 'reinforces exclusion'.[76] Interestingly, there was a degree of audience resistance, including from *banlieue* youth, to what some perceived as the excessive obscenity in *La Haine*'s dialogue, as discussed in Chapter 3.[77]

Race relations and representations, French-style

If the setting, characters and language of *La Haine* dictate that we place it in a tradition of French representations of the *banlieue*, it is equally important to consider the film – which features a multi-ethnic trio of central protagonists – in terms of race and ethnicity in France and their portrayal in French cinema. *La Haine* pinpoints the well-documented racism of the French police, implicitly – for instance, images in the opening montage (see Chapter 2) – and explicitly. For example, Saïd and Hubert are subjected to brutal racist humiliation by two policemen. Yet, despite such scenes, and the beating of young *Beur* Abdel that triggers off the action, the film rapidly shifts to general police violence, and it foregrounds its cohesive *black blanc beur* central trio against the police and 'bourgeois society'. This is an aspect of the film that has given rise to significant debate, some arguing that *La Haine* sweeps racism under the carpet, others denouncing the 'politically correct' but 'unrealistic' *black blanc beur* trio (further details can be found in Chapter 3). These claims will be examined in the analysis of the film and of its reception. For the moment, I want to ask how the representation of ethnicity in *La Haine* relates to social life in France and other films and media images.

Race, ethnicity and citizenship in France

La Haine emerged in 1990s France, at a time when multi-ethnicity was on the rise and racism omnipresent, yet racial integration was noticeably higher than in Anglo-American countries – for example, in terms of mixed marriages. This 'French paradox' derives from a combination of historical factors: the French Republican conception of citizenship, colonial history and various layers of government action.

Born of the French Revolution, the Jacobin notion of equality posits that differences of race, religion and gender are subsumed under the identity of the citizen, a proposition duplicated in the secular state education system, which insists that religion remains in the private domain – especially since the separation of (Roman Catholic) Church and state in 1905. Traditionally, the 'French model' of citizenship was based on soil (*jus soli*) combined with residence, as opposed to birth (*jus sanguinis*), as in the 'German model'. Until recently children born on French soil automatically qualified for French nationality. This has successfully integrated waves of immigrants (Jewish, Polish, Italian, Spanish and Portuguese), but also – unlike the British/US model – produced a lack of recognition of multi-culturalism, perceived as divisive and conducive to a ghetto mentality.

In the 1950s immigrants from Algeria, Morocco and Tunisia pre-dominated, but since the 1980s people from sub-Saharan Africa, then South-East Asia and Turkey, have made up the greatest numbers. However, because of colonial ties between France and Africa, and the growing numbers of descendants of North and sub-Saharan African immigrants, the latter are the main issue when it comes to the *banlieues*. Mass immigration from Africa began in the 1950s, consisting of male migrant workers employed in unskilled factory jobs. Most stayed and brought their families, and more came even after the government officially stopped immigration and encouraged a return 'home' (*aide au retour*) from 1974. Their children, who came of age in the 1980s, made up the first generation of '*Beurs*' and 'blacks'. As we saw in the microcosm of Chanteloup-les-Vignes, while their parents were the victims of capitalist exploitation during the economic boom, they found themselves unemployed. They also experienced the ambivalences of a dual identity, torn between their French upbringing and the culture of their parents.

The 1980s also saw the rise of both *beur* militancy and the fascist National Front of Jean-Marie Le Pen, who used immigration from Africa (as well as anti-Semitism) as an electoral platform. François Mitterrand's Socialist government, which came to power in 1981, while by no means eradicating racism, supported anti-racist initiatives such as SOS-Racisme (it is in this context that *beur* films emerged). Nevertheless, because of colonial history, especially the violent Algerian war of independence, immigrants from the Maghreb remained the main targets of hostility. According to Alec Hargreaves, 80% of violent racist acts and 90% of racist murders in France target *Beurs*.[78] The return of the right to power in 1993 polarised immigration issues further, especially with the new immigration laws steered by right-wing Interior Minister Charles Pasqua (whose comically made-up portrait as a *Beur* can be seen on Darty's wall in *La Haine*, near a large portrait of

The *black blanc beur* trio (Saïd, Vinz, Hubert)

Hip-hop culture: the DJ

Hip-hop culture: break-dancing

Bob Marley). The 'Pasqua laws' of 1993 restricted access to French citizenship, which was now no longer automatically based on place of birth, creating a climate of racial fear.

Yet, at the same time, youths of all colours brought up and educated together, and sharing the same environment, have much in common. The *cité*, as Michel Cadé points out, paradoxically acts as a site of racial integration 'from below'.[79] The *cité* portrayed in *La Haine* is typical of many others at the time in displaying a higher degree of ethnic mixing than American inner city ghettos,[80] even if, as we have seen, this was not the case in the real Chanteloup-les-Vignes. In French society at large, a degree of *beur* and black integration has taken place, through work and mixed marriages.[81] This is in evidence in various spheres of society. There is a growing '*beurgeoisie*' and black middle class and an expanding group of successful *beur* and black writers, sportsmen and women, artists and stars – the writer Tahar Ben Jelloun and the footballer Zinedine Zidane being the most famous. While stereotyping remains the norm for most black and *beur* actors (see Saïd Taghmaoui and Hubert Koundé's post-*Haine* careers in Chapter 3), some have forged successful careers. Smaïn, Djamel Debouzze, Gad Elmaleh and Dieudonné are household names as stage and television comics (and in films drawing on their television persona), while Sami Nacery became a star after the enormous success of the *Taxi* series of comic action films. Another example of ethnic mix particularly relevant to *La Haine* is hip-hop culture.

Hip-hop culture has been particularly successful since the early 1980s in France. Unsurprisingly, young blacks are prominent in French rap groups, which mostly emanate from the Paris and Marseille *banlieues*, and hip-hop has been a vehicle for group identity and solidarity as well as cultural rebellion. More unusual is the significant presence of *Beurs* and whites. As André Prévos puts it: 'The ethnic diversity of rappers in France is now a widely recognized fact.'[82] Steve Cannon also points out that the expression *black blanc beur* – a pun on the French flag: *bleu blanc rouge* – had had currency in hip-hop circles from the 1980s.[83] The expression was thus in use long before *La Haine,* and, indeed, before the *black blanc beur* French football team won the World Cup in 1998. Hip-hop culture, in all its manifestations (rap music, break-dancing and tagging), can be seen and heard in *La Haine*, and its presence is also materialised through casting. For instance, Solo Dicko (who plays the character Santo) is a member of the band 'Assassin', and the break-dancers were recruited among real dancers. The racial/ethnic mix of *La Haine*'s central trio and of the policemen and break-dancers is thus, for the mid-1990s, reasonably realistic.

Two last points on ethnicity and *La Haine*. First, there is the film's accent on Jewish cultural difference. As already noted, this is an autobiographical gesture on the part of Kassovitz, who recognises that such families are atypical in the *cités*: Ashkenazi Jewish families from Eastern Europe tend to be located in central Paris or in middle-class suburbs. On the other hand, the *grand ensemble* of Sarcelles was (and still is) host to numerous Sephardic Jews – mostly *pieds noirs*, the colonial settlers repatriated from North Africa after the wars of independence. Kassovitz's insistence on Jewishness counters the reductive view of a 'white republican Frenchness' that would be monolithically opposed to immigrants of African origins (a notion often found in Anglo-American writing on the topic). Second, the racial situation in France has changed significantly since 1995, with shifts in the pattern of immigration, in particular the influx of immigrants from China and Turkey and from the Balkans. The rise of Islamic fundamentalism, exacerbated by 11 September 2001, has increased both anti-Arab racism and part-Arab-fuelled anti-Semitism (at the time of writing Jewish property is routinely desecrated and French Jewish emigration to Israel is on the rise). While there is continued integration, descendants of originally African origin penetrating all levels of society (including, finally, the government), there is in the poor layers of society a greater rejection of the traditional French integrationist model, as well as a worsening of the image of the *cités* insofar as they are seen as recruitment grounds for Islamic terrorists. Thus the ethnic 'French paradox' of the post-colonial period continues.

Between Spike Lee *and* cinéma beur

While it portrays a very rooted French environment, *La Haine* appeals explicitly to America in filmic terms – the work of Spike Lee, black 'gangsta' movies such as *Menace II Society* (the Hughes Brothers, 1993) and *Boyz 'N the Hood* (John Singleton, 1991) rather than French films. From *Do The Right Thing*, it quotes the presence of a DJ and an altercation with an Asian shopkeeper (which also occurs in *Menace II Society*) and indirectly suggests riots as the 'inevitable' outcome of the tensions depicted in the film. Though music is used sparingly, rap and Bob Marley on the soundtrack, break-dancing and the young men's clothes accentuate the parallels with black films. Yet, ironically, the main difference between *La Haine* and its American models is in the treatment of race. The world of *Menace II Society* and *Boyz 'N the Hood* is all-black and confrontational; that of *La Haine* is mixed and consensual. *Do The Right Thing* concentrates on violent racial conflict, *La Haine* focuses on the common fate of mixed-race groups. Only Joseph B. Vasquez's *Hangin' With the Homeboys* (1991) offers a similar format, as it features mixed (Latino and African-American) characters who get on well together and present a unified front against outsiders. Despite American *cinematic* sources, *La Haine* is *sociologically* in line with French representations of race and ethnicity, especially those of *beur* films.

Cinéma beur – loosely understood as films made by *Beurs* about *beur* characters and topics[84] – emerged in the mid-1980s, as a set of low- to medium-budget narrative films spearheaded by Mehdi Charef's *Le Thé au Harem d'Archimède* in 1985. As the largest group among French immigrants, it is not surprising that *Beurs* should produce the most substantial and successful group of 'ethnic' filmmakers in France. *Beur* films echoed the public visibility of *Beurs* on the French scene discussed above, and they represented a form of expression for the *beur* community. The term '*beur*' as already discussed, is not 'innocent'. Equally problematic is the category of '*beur* filmmakers'. As Carrie Tarr, author of the most substantial study of *beur* cinema, says: 'This type of grouping runs counter to the desire of the filmmakers themselves, who, understandably, do not want to be labelled in terms of their ethnic origins.'[85] Nevertheless, recurrent themes and images in the films arguably justify such a grouping. With few exceptions, *beur* films of the 1980s and 1990s are located in the Parisian *cités* and they concentrate on its young male inhabitants. *La Haine* clearly echoes this tradition, including in its gender bias, as it does the *beur* films' approach to ethnicity. *Beur* films aimed to counter racist representations of *Beurs* as negative 'others' – criminals and drug dealers in mainstream French films, in particular thrillers such as *La Balance* (1982), *Police* (1985) and *L627* (1992). Yet, as Christian Bosséno noted of 1980s *beur* films, 'The theme of racism, which lay at the heart of the [1960s and 1970s] films made by North African (and indeed black) immigrants, is now virtually absent from their works. [...] All [young characters] suffer the same raw deal to an equal degree.'[86] Indeed, *Le Thé au harem d'Archimède, Hexagone, Raï, Douce France* and others, while they explore with sympathy the difficulties of the young *Beurs*' dual identity, also put the accent on the social 'raw deal' (*la galère*) suffered by all *banlieue* youth, regardless of skin colour. Accordingly, narratives focus on mixed-race groups of young men and their common problems, compounded by the real and symbolic absence of fathers – as we will see, *La Haine* fits squarely within this tradition. Interestingly, audience reactions to the film from young spectators from the *banlieue* echo this: opinions were varied, but they addressed issues of class, language and location, not race. Similarly, journalistic and academic reactions to the film on the French side have paid little attention to race and ethnicity, as opposed to the systematic explorations of this topic from Anglo-American writers (both are detailed in Chapter 3). This phenomenon is not limited to *La Haine*. Michel Marie's collection on the *jeune cinéma français* (discussed below) includes interviews and articles on *beur* films and filmmakers, but makes little of their ethnic origins. In a more explicit way, René Prédal claims, 'the French situation is not that of the United States and… I want to study films without being concerned with the sex or skin colour of their authors'.[87] Whether this attitude is evidence of blindness or integration is subject to the same debate as the films themselves.

Jeune cinéma français and the 'new realism'

So far we have discussed how La Haine belongs to contexts related to the banlieue, its language, race relations and the representation of race and ethnicity. We also saw how the film was the product of a young team and how Kassovitz's personal development led him to the point of making it. Finally, we need to go back to the wider cinematic context and see how La Haine fits within an important trend in French cinema of the 1990s, the so-called jeune cinéma français.

The year 1995 was good for French cinema. Out of a total production of 141 films, four French films were among the top five at the French box office, and six in the top ten.[88] Most of the successful French titles were popular comedies and heritage films. By contrast, La Haine was a contemporary realist and young film, and it was perceived as such. At the Cannes festival, for instance, it was described as 'far ahead of the other "young" films in the competition'.[89] La Haine signalled the arrival of the jeune cinéma français in the mainstream, beyond its normal cinephile circle.

The question of a 'young' French cinema has been on the critical agenda ever since the new wave introduced youth as a supreme factor in cinematic innovation. Since the 1960s critics of French cinema have been keen to find successors to the original new wave, and various 'new new waves' have been detected. In the 1990s the expression seemed genuinely justified by the appearance of a significant group of young filmmakers, whose collective identity was strong enough to generate the label of jeune cinéma français, a concept and practice explored in three recent French books and discussed in several works in English.[90] In April 2004 Jean-Pierre Jeancolas opened a conference on 1990s French cinema in London with the provocative notion that the 'jeune cinéma français' did not exist, and yet proceeded to detail its practitioners and the conditions for its existence.[91]

What is undeniable is a remarkably high number of first films (over one-third of 1990s production); according to Jeancolas, 329 new French filmmakers made their debut in the 1990s, turning out 293 first films between 1988 and 2002, the starting point for this renaissance being generally agreed to be Eric Rochant's 1989 Un monde sans pitié (produced by Lazennec, as we saw). The films are critically supported by journals such as Cahiers du *cinéma, Positif* and *Les Inrockuptibles,* as well as by the industry through prizes to first films and 'young' filmmakers. Many of the latter are alumni of the FEMIS or École Louis Lumière film schools, and many started working in short films, an area that has become particularly active again. The 'young' films are generously helped by state/industry finance (one-third of them obtained the *avance sur recettes*) and 'young' television channels such as Arte and, especially, Canal+. In addition, a new breed of producers supports their efforts: apart from Lazennec, which we have discussed, the most prominent are Noé Productions and Rezo films.

Within *jeune cinéma français* several 'families' of filmmakers overlap, covering different genres and preoccupations. Yet some common points emerge. To simplify, in order to understand Kassovitz's place within it, I shall divide the *jeune cinéma français* into two major trends. On the one hand, there is the 'French auteurs' trend, with filmmakers such as Xavier Beauvois, Arnaud Desplechin, Sandrine Veysset, Laetitia Masson, Bruno Dumont – young men but also many women who make 'small' auteur films appealing to a select cinephile audience, financed predominantly with the help of the *avance sur recettes* and often the Arte channel. On the other hand, there is the genre-oriented – and more masculine – cinema of Kassovitz, Gaspar Noé, Jan Kounen and Christophe Gans. These young men make more spectacular, violent and potentially mainstream films, which appeal to a broader young audience. Indeed, Kassovitz has voiced his dislike of 'over-intellectual' and 'boring' French auteur cinema in several interviews.[92] Although the aesthetics of the genre-oriented *jeune cinéma français* are in opposition to those of television, their finance often comes from Canal+. These filmmakers are also more 'American' in their outlook and influences – a 'generation born of Martin Scorsese', as Nicolas Boukhrief puts it. They challenge the French auteur tradition in wanting 'to make the kind of cinema that travels round the world and not only through embassies'.[93]

Across this division, what connects the disparate films of the *jeune cinéma français* is their address to social issues in French society as well as to characters and backgrounds hitherto considered 'marginal'. This makes it a markedly different kind of cinema from the narcissistic personal relationships in bourgeois milieux favoured by many traditional French auteur films, on the one hand, and the sleek 1980s *cinéma du look.* The critical consensus is that the young filmmakers of the 1990s 'share an engagement with social problems'. And, even if 'they don't all address the hard side of the *fracture sociale*',[94] they at least, in Prédal's terms, show that 'times have changed: what is interesting happens in this peripheral social group and no longer at the centre of the *petite bourgeoisie*'.[95]

The films of the *jeune cinéma français*, then, are perceived as offering a 'new realism'. They are almost entirely shot on location, frequently depict working-class, underclass or 'marginal' protagonists, often in ordinary surroundings. In a departure from Paris-based French cinema, there is also a strong emphasis on 'unglamorous' regions such as the North. Yet this does not mean that the *jeune cinéma français* can be called realist in a classic sense. As Vincent Amiel points out, the films are frequently marked, in their approach to 'the real', by either genre or stylistic distanciation, as well as a focus on young characters who retreat from the 'adult' world or the world of work; a startling number of films focus on mentally disturbed, ill-adapted marginals.[96] Nor is this cinema political in the sense of depicting organised, future-oriented action or of being informed by well-defined ideology: Jean-François Richet's Marxist *État des lieux* is one of the rare films that is. This retreat from the political (in the traditional sense of the term), already observed in the 1980s after the explicitly political cinema of the 1970s, clearly reflects changing attitudes to actual political engagement. In the context of the collapse of the Communist Party and the waning of trade union power, by the mid-1990s politics had moved on to different forms of action – for example, engagement with individual cases and humanitarian causes: police *bavures*, torture, AIDS, landmines: in 1997 Kassovitz contributed a short film to *Lumières sur un massacre*, an anti-landmine film. The most famous humanitarian cause in France was the 1996/1997 affair of the '*sans papiers*', in which illegal immigrants ('those without [identity] papers') were threatened with expulsion; the 'Debré law' subsequently also threatened French citizens who helped house these immigrants. A group of 66 filmmakers – among them Mathieu Kassovitz – signed a petition on 11 February 1997 calling for 'civil disobedience' by stating that they had housed '*sans papiers*'. In this perspective, the films of the *jeune cinéma français* may be said to exist in a 'post-ideology' era, in which traditional politics are replaced by individual – often violent – revolt, or a retreat into the family, friendship or fantasy. It is in this sense that we will examine in what way *La Haine* is a 'political' film.

In his discussion of the 'new realism' in French cinema of the 1990s, Phil Powrie finds it difficult to place *La Haine*. The film is seen both as evidence of a 'preoccupation with social and political affairs' and 'not particularly representative of the "return to the real"'.[97] In truth, these contradictions are at the heart of the film, which merges social concerns, genre cinema and auteur preoccupations – a smart and timely mix that explains its explosive success and why it came to represent the cutting edge of the *jeune cinéma français*, even as it departed from many of its concerns. It is now time to turn to the film itself.

Notes

1   Interview with Mathieu Kassovitz, Vincent, Rémy, *Télérama*, 31 May 1995.
2   'Interview with Mathieu Kassovitz', in M. Ciment and N. Herpe (eds), *Projections 9: French Film-makers on Film-making, in association with Positif*. London and New York, Faber and Faber, 1999, p. 184.
3   Apiou, Virginie, interview with Mathieu Kassovitz, *Synopsis*, 29, 2004, p. 23. Kassovitz also says that as an adolescent he won 200 science fiction books and read them all.
4   'Y'a d'la haine...y'a d'lamour – Mathieu Kassovitz', *Studio Magazine*, special issue Cannes 1995, p. 111.
5   J.D., 'interview du fanzine *Steadycam*', available online on Mathieu Kassovitz's official website: http://www.mathieukassovitz.com/itw/steadycam.htm, copyright 1998/2004 (accessed June 2004).
6   'Y'a d'la haine...y'a d'lamour – Mathieu Kassovitz', p. 107.
7   J.D., 'interview du fanzine *Steadycam*'.
8   In a 2001 interview Kassovitz says that he and Mauduech split up, but later on got back together. They have a child, called Carmen. In 'Mathieu Kassovitz by Nicole Kidman', *Interview*, October 2001, p. 233.
9   The actress is credited as Eloïse Rauth in *Métisse* and Heloïse Rauth in *La Haine*.
10   The CNC is the body that allocates financial help to French films under a variety of schemes, the most important of which being the *avance sur recettes*.
11   Interview with Mathieu Kassovitz, *Studio Magazine*, June 1995, p. 45.
12   Quoted in Riou, Alain, *Le Nouvel Observateur*, 25 May 1995.
13   'Interview with Nicolas Boukhrief', in M. Marie (ed.), *Le jeune cinéma français*. Paris, Nathan, 1998, p. 39.
14   Riou, *Le Nouvel Observateur*, 25 May 1995.
15   Rossignon, Christophe, *Le Film Français*, 22 September 1995, p. 11.
16   From the Canal+ documentary on the 'making of' *La Haine*, Canal+ DVD, *La Haine*, 2001.
17   J.D., 'interview du fanzine *Steadycam*'.
18   Danel, Isabelle, interview with Vincent Cassel, *Télérama*, 3 July 1996, pp. 36–38.
19   *France-Soir*, 31 May 1995.
20   Rémy, interview with Mathieu Kassovitz.
21   Danel, Isabelle, interview with Saïd Taghmaoui, *Télérama*, 3 July 1996, pp. 36–38.
22   Bourguignon, Thomas and Tobin, Yann, interview with Mathieu Kassovitz, *Positif*, No 412, June 1995, p. 8 (this section of the interview is missing from the English translation in the *Projections 9* book quoted elsewhere in this chapter).
23   J.D., 'interview du fanzine *Steadycam*'.
24   *L'Express*, 11 May 1995.
25   *Télérama*, 31 May 1995, p. 42.
26   'Tournage: *La Haine*', *Studio Magazine*, January 1995, p. 91.
27   'Budgets prévisionnels comparés', *Studio Magazine*, special issue 'L'Année cinéma 95', pp. 122–123.
28   Rémy, interview with Mathieu Kassovitz.
29   Ibid.
30   Dumas, Frédérique, in M. Marie (ed.), *Le jeune cinéma français*, p. 52; Rossignon, *Le Film Français*, 22 September 1995, p. 11.
31   *Studio Magazine*, 'hors série', December 1995, p. 103.

32   Rossignon, *Le Film Français*, 22 September 1995, p. 11.
33   J.D., 'interview du fanzine *Steadycam*'. According to Mathieu Kassovitz's audio commentary (Canal+ DVD of *La Haine*, 2001), one or two copies entirely in colour were distributed in Italy.
34   'Interview with Mathieu Kassovitz', in Ciment and Herpe (eds), *Projections 9*, p. 188.
35   Kassovitz, Mathieu, DVD audio commentary, *La Haine*, Canal+ 'Kulte' series, 2001.
36   *L'Express*, 11 May 1995.
37   Interview with Mathieu Kassovitz, *Première*, June 1995, p. 106.
38   *L'Express*, 11 May 1995.
39   Rémy, interview with Mathieu Kassovitz.
40   *L'Express*, 11 May 1995.
41   Rémy, interview with Mathieu Kassovitz.
42   J.D., 'interview du fanzine *Steadycam*'.
43   Pantel, Monique, interview with Mathieu Kassovitz, *France-Soir*, 26 May 1995.
44   'Interview with Mathieu Kassovitz', in Ciment and Herpe (eds), *Projections 9*, p. 191.
45   Examples can be seen in the 'making of' documentary on the Canal+ DVD of *La Haine*.
46   'Interview with Mathieu Kassovitz', in Ciment and Herpe (eds), *Projections 9*, p. 184.
47   Hargreaves, Alec G., 'Violent changes: the Beurs and the banlieues', in F. Aitsiselmi (ed.), *Black, Blanc, Beur: Youth Language and Identity in France*, Interface: Bradford Study in Language, Culture and Society no. 5. Bradford, Bradford University Press, 2000, p. 12.
48   '*Fracture sociale*' is an expression coined by sociologist Emmanuel Todd, and refers to the concern that a section of the population, including a high proportion of immigrants, is disenfranchised from mainstream society, leading to a rupture of the social fabric.
49   Luce Vigo argues a different etymology, whereby *banlieue* means a banishment (ban) one *lieue* from the city (Vigo, Luce, 'Ce cinéma qui habite la banlieue', *Regards*, September 1995). However, the *Grand Robert* dictionary seems unequivocal about the first meaning, of a band situated immediately outside the city, and under its jurisdiction.
50   Reader, Keith, 'After the riot', *Sight and Sound*, 5, (11), 1995, p. 12.
51   Robache, Thomas and Saragoussi, Pierre, *Banlieues: tant que ça tiendra*. Paris, Denoël, 1998, p. 81.
52   Vieillard-Baron, Hervé, 'Chanteloup-les-Vignes, le risque du ghetto', *Esprit*, November 1987, p. 10.
53   Zakya Daoud, 'Interview with Pierre Cardo', *Panoramiques*, Special issue on the *banlieue*, 2 December 1993, p. 182.
54   Vieillard-Baron, *Esprit*, November 1987, p. 13.
55   Ibid., p. 21.
56   Vieillard-Baron, Hervé, 'L'Architecture', *Panoramiques*, special issue on the *banlieue*, 2 December 1993, p. 81.
57   See Maspéro, François, *Les Passagers du Roissy-Express*. Paris, Éditions du Seuil, 1990 (translated by P. Jones as *Roissy Express*. London, Verso, 1994) and Garnier, Jean-Pierre, *Des Barbares dans la cité: de la tyrannie du marché à la violence urbaine*. Paris, Flammarion, 1996.

58 *Libération*, 17 January 2000, p. 18.

59 'Le retour des tribus', *Marianne*, 15–21 February 1999, pp. 44–45.

60 Nouchi, Franck, *Le Monde*, 28 October 1995, p. 7; Phillipe, Bernard, *Le Monde*, 19 June 1996, p. 7.

61 See, in particular, issue no 59/60 of *Les Cahiers de la cinémathèque* (February 1994) and Vigo, Luce, 'Ce cinéma qui habite la banlieue', *Regards*, September 1995.

62 Baldizzone, José, 'Carné, Blier et Rohmer vont…"Loin…en banlieue"', *Les Cahiers de la cinémathèque*, 59/60, 1994, p. 113.

63 Prédal, René, *Le Jeune Cinéma français*. Paris, Nathan, 2002, p. 116.

64 Taranger, Marie-Claude, 'Télévision et "western urbain", enjeux et nuances de l'information sur les banlieues', *Les Cahiers de la cinémathèque*, 59/60, February 1994, p. 60.

65 Ibid., p. 65

66 Ibid., pp. 62–63.

67 Barbancey, Pierre, *L'Humanité*, 17 May 1997.

68 Wolinski, Natacha, *InfoMatin*, 31 May 1995.

69 Ferreboeuf, Georges, quoted in 'Médias et banlieues: la haine?', http://www.lyoncapitale, 1996 (accessed May 1998).

70 Maspéro, *Les Passagers du Roissy-Express*.

71 Didier, Daeninckx, *Zapping*. Paris, Denoël, 1992, pp. 79–92.

72 Documentary on the 'making of' of *La Haine*, Canal+DVD, 2001.

73 Taranger, Marie-Claude, 'Télévision et "western urbain"', p. 64.

74 Gilles, Edmond, interview with Karim Dridi, *L'Humanité*, 14 September 1995, p. 24.

75 Merle, Pierre, *Argot, Verlan et Tchatches*. Toulouse, Éditions Milan, 1997, pp. 50–53.

76 Begag, Azouz, 'L'enfermement linguistique ou la langue des banlieues comme facteur d'assignation sociale', in F. Aitsiselmi (ed.), *Black, Blanc, Beur*, p. 5.

77 *Télérama*, 28 June 1995, pp. 25–27.

78 Hargreaves, 'Violent Changes', p. 12. One issue that most visibly concentrated the 'fear' of a rising tide of immigration, whipped up by the National Front, was – and still is – that of the headscarf (hijab) worn by young Islamic women, an 'ostentatious' religious sign considered illegal at school under the secular French education system.

79 Cadé, Michel, 'Des immigrés dans les banlieues', *Les Cahiers de la cinémathèque*, 59/60, p. 126.

80 For a comparison between the French and American situation, see in particular Wacquant, Loïs, 'De l'Amérique comme utopie à l'envers', in P. Boudieu (ed.), *La Misère du monde*. Paris, Éditions du Seuil, 1993.

81 The 1999 census indicates that 9.6% of marriages were with a 'foreign spouse' (which does not include French people of foreign origins). See also Todd, Emmanuel, *Le Destin des immigrés: assimilation et ségrégation dans les démocraties modernes*. Paris, Éditions du Seuil, 1994.

82 Prévos, André J.M., 'Two Decades of rap in France: emergence, developments, prospects', in A.-P. Durand (ed.), *Black, Blanc, Beur: rap music and hip-hop culture in the Francophone world*. Lanham, MD, Scarecrow Press, 2002, p. 5.

83 Cannon, Steve, 'Paname City rapping: B-boys in the banlieues and beyond', in A.G. Hargreaves and M. McKinney (eds), *Post-Colonial Cultures in France*. London and New York, Routledge, 1997, p. 163.

84   See Bosséno, Christian, 'Immigrant cinema: national cinema – the case of *beur* film', in R. Dyer and G. Vincendeau (eds), *Popular European Cinema*. London, Routledge, 1992.

85   Tarr, Carrie, introduction to *Beur and Banlieue filmmaking in France*. Manchester, Manchester University Press, forthcoming.

86   Bosséno, Christian, 'Immigrant cinema', p. 48.

87   Prédal, *Le Jeune Cinéma français*, p. 140.

88   *Ciné-Passions: 7e art et industrie de 1945 à 2000*. Paris, Éditions Dixit/CNC, 2000, p. 102.

89   Coppermann, Annie, *Les Echos*, 31 May 1995.

90   Trémois, Claude-Marie, *Les Enfants de la liberté: le jeune cinéma français des années 90*. Paris, Éditions du Seuil, 1995. M. Marie's collection of interviews and short pieces *Le jeune cinéma français*. R. Prédal's book *Le Jeune Cinéma français*. Powrie, Phil, *French Cinema in the 1990s: Continuity and Difference*. Oxford, Oxford University Press, 1999.

91   Jeancolas, Jean-Pierre, introductory speech, conference on 'Studies in French Cinema', French Institute, London, 16 April 2004.

92   For instance, Charity, interview with Mathieu Kassovitz, pp. 26–27.

93   'Interview with Nicolas Boukhrief', in M. Marie (ed.), *Le jeune cinéma français*, p. 43.

94   Prédal, in M. Marie (ed.), *Le jeune cinéma français*, p. 6.

95   Prédal, *Le Jeune Cinéma français*, p. 139.

96   Amiel, Vincent, 'Une nouvelle génération', *Esprit*, Decembre 1997, pp. 100–102.

97   Powrie, Phil, 'Heritage, history and "new realism": French cinema in the 1990s', in Powrie (ed.), *French Cinema in the 1990s*, pp. 16–17.

2   Narrative, style and ideology in *La Haine*

Everything had to seem real and yet be graphically interesting.

Mathieu Kassovitz[1]

Tension and randomness: the narrative structure

La Haine follows a day in the life of a group of three ethnically diverse young men – a *Beur*, Saïd, the Jewish Vinz and Hubert, who is black – from a deprived suburban *cité*. The film starts the morning after riots provoked by the police accidentally wounding a young *Beur*, Abdel. It then charts the bored, aimless life of the three protagonists – who are neither at school nor at work – in a series of more or less violent encounters, in particular with the police, first in the *banlieue* then in Paris, ending in a decisive episode of shocking violence (for more details, see the detailed Synopsis at the beginning of this book and a breakdown of sequences in Appendix 2).

At the time of the film's release, Mathieu Kassovitz put forward the notion that his film was 'unstructured', a series of disconnected scenes in a film in which 'nothing happens'.[2] He claimed that 'each scene constitutes a short film in itself'[3] and that, in the Paris section in particular, 'there is no real continuity, so we could do anything we liked'.[4] This is, to some extent, the experience of the first-time viewer, and this style of narration appears appropriate to the fragmented, random lives of the protagonists. Close scrutiny, however, shows that *La Haine* is, on the contrary, a minutely structured and classically coherent film.

Symbolic divisions and dramatic structure

La Haine is, first of all, structured around a strong geographical and temporal dichotomy, between daytime *banlieue* and night-time Paris – a division that many writers have, rightly, seen as symbolic. For Martine Beugnet, for instance, this duality alone makes the film an 'allegory of the *fracture sociale*'.[5] Secondly, there is the cyclical aspect of the narrative, whereby the televised documentary violence that opens the film alludes to the 'cycle of violence' in the real-life *banlieue* – at the same time as it prefigures the fictional violence that concludes the film the next morning, thus looping back to the beginning. In plot terms, a police *bavure* (the accidental shooting of Abdel) provoked the fictional riots that took place before the film opens, and another *bavure* – the shooting of Vinz – concludes it, again suggesting a loop, an endless repetition of such events. This cyclical structure is itself duplicated at the level of the smaller units that make up the narrative.

Internally, episodes are organised around a series of mini-climaxes, followed by periods of calm in the *cité* section, while in Paris virtually all the scenes end with some violent occurrence. After the credits sequence over the opening montage (sequence 1 – numbers refer to the breakdown in Appendix 2) the first half of the film, set in the *cité*, is organised in eight sequences, which can themselves be grouped in three larger units, of roughly equal length. The first block, made of sequences 2 and 3, in which we meet Saïd, Vinz and Hubert and follow them on the rooftop (*c.* 13 minutes), ends with the police disbanding the youths. In the second block – sequences 4, 5 and 6 (*c.* 14 minutes) – we follow the heroes hanging around and telling stories, discover Vinz has stolen the gun and watch their attempt to visit Abdel in hospital, ending with Saïd's arrest, his release from the police station and an argument between the three friends about the gun. Block 3 – sequences 7, 8 and 9 (c. 13 minutes) – has us follow Hubert at home, listen to a DJ, see Vinz go for the shopkeeper and botch Saïd's haircut, watch break-dancing, and finally witness a violent fight provoked by Abdel's brother and brutally quashed by the CRS[6] (riot police), our heroes escaping through the cellars and jumping on a train to Paris. Each of the three blocks ends up in violence and police involvement. In the Paris section, the first sequence (10) is the only peaceful one, during which the three young men listen to an old man telling his story. After that, all the sequences end in, or are structured around, violence (fighting (11, 16), shooting (13, 16), arguing (14), fleeing the police (15), being assaulted by them (12)), thus preparing the spectator for the truly violent climax of the end (17). This narrative organisation calls for further scrutiny.

First, despite the fact that it is the *banlieue* that is supposed to be violent, the frequency of violence increases in the Paris section – although it is individual violence as opposed to the collective violence of the *cité*. The second half thus shows the three heroes 'carrying' *banlieue* aggression with them to Paris, highlighting their greater exclusion from the city centre. But this feature is also a function of classical dramatic construction. The first half of the film needs to spend more time establishing the protagonists and their environments – thus sequences 2, 4, 5, 7 and 8 depict the boys 'hanging out' and meeting a variety of characters. The handling of time is interesting. While the two halves in the *cité* and in Paris are of roughly equal screen time, the compression of time within some sequences is occasionally unrealistic: sequences 6, 7 and part of 8 allocate just over one hour of 'real' time (15:57 to 17:04 according to the clock that regularly appears in the film) to a substantial series of events: the hospital visit, Saïd's arrest and release, Hubert at home, the DJ scene, Vinz cutting Saïd's hair – practically impossible in one hour and seven minutes. Similarly, between 17:04 and 18:22 (just over one hour and a quarter) the heroes are supposed to hang out and watch break-dancing, fight with the CRS, escape through the cellars and make their getaway to central Paris. This may seem like nit-picking, but it shows that the point of the clock is not to provide a realistic account of time passing but to serve other functions, which we will turn to shortly.

A clock, a gun and stories

We have seen that the film is strongly structured along a dichotomy in space and time and according to a cyclical logic at various levels. Cutting across these patterns, *La Haine* follows traditional causality: an event (the riots of the night before) supplies the initial motivation for the three protagonists' journey – their desire to see Abdel in hospital, Saïd's brief imprisonment, Vinz's desire for revenge. Later, Abdel's brother rekindles this plot by firing at the police, triggering off a mini-version of the riots and propelling the protagonists to Paris, and, finally, Abdel's death leads indirectly to the violent finale. Under this major line of causality, other more subtle ones operate: the visit to the fence Darty sends them on to Astérix (since Darty does not have the money Saïd needs to collect); the encounter with Santo in the break-dancing episode initiates Vinz's visit to the boxing match, and – in his imagination – the killing of the nightclub bouncer. Thus we can see that, contrary to Kassovitz's assertion that 'there [is] no plot, it's like a diary or a news report',[7] *La Haine* is extremely tightly plotted.

The journey of the protagonists also follows a familiar kind of cinematic plot, that of the road movie. Although their journey is geographically short, our three heroes, as in a road movie, are constantly on the move (walking, running, on the train), passing through diverse locations and having numerous encounters on the way: they clash with relatives, officials, policemen, journalists, a shopkeeper, a neighbour, a concierge, patrons at an art gallery, a taxi driver, a man on an escalator, skinheads, not to mention each other. Many of these encounters are dramatic or violent. As Myrto Konstantarakos points out of the *banlieue* film in general: 'The trip [to Paris] is never easy, as if the distance between the two places were immense.'[8] Clearly the physical journey of the protagonists is meant to have other – social, psychological or moral – kinds of significance, in this case leading to a tragic ending. In this respect, it is worth noting an interesting difference between *La Haine* and similar youth-oriented American films, especially *Hangin' With the Homeboys*, in which, as we have already discussed, an ethnically mixed group of young men (two blacks, two Latinos) from the Bronx spend a night 'on the town' and encounter various forms of exclusion – such as being thrown out of a party and getting into trouble with the police. The journey of the heroes into Manhattan through the night parallels a moral trajectory: each has a 'problem' that the narrative will solve. For instance, one of them hesitates between improving himself by taking up a scholarship or continuing a life of fun with the 'homeboys'; he opts for the scholarship. This ending, as is traditional in American cinema, offers the characters a moral redemption. In *La Haine,* however, no such personal redemption, learning or problem solving occurs. The heroes have no personal goal and they start and end in the same place (Hubert's hopes of progress through boxing are shown to be already shattered in one of the first scenes of the film). Vinz gives up his gun but is still caught in violence. The tragic ending has a collective social dimension, rather than an individual moral one.

Finally, I want to note three narrative devices that contribute to the fine narrative mesh of the film: the clock, the gun, the telling of stories. As hinted above, the time counter is more testimony to the film's manipulation of time than a realistic account of the characters' movements, and a certain amount of adjustment is taking place. The counter appears arbitrarily and corresponds neither to regular blocks of time nor to the film's internal structure (some sequences contain two appearances of the clock, others none). This apparent randomness contributes to the realistic effect of the film: 17:04 seems more improvised and therefore more 'real' than 17:00. The clock, with its loud ticking, gives the film urgency, the impression of a 'countdown'[9] exacerbated at the end, where, for the first and last time, we see the digits move, from 6:00 to 6:01. In *La Haine* as in Agnès Varda's 1961 *Cléo de 5 à 7* (a film that also does not correspond to its proclaimed 'real time'), apart from quite obviously foregrounding the *theme* of time the material appearance of a clock at certain intervals, by rupturing the fiction, exhibits the author's signature on the film text.

We are introduced to the gun – a Smith and Wesson 44 Magnum lost by a policeman during the riots – early on in the film, in the *cité* rooftop sequence (3). Thematically, the gun obviously foregrounds violence and a host of related themes. As a cop's gun, it is symbolic of many police *bavures* (Makome M'Bowole – the trigger for Kassovitz's script – was shot in the head). It whips up Vinz's latent aggression, as the symbol of the violent patriarchal power he and his friends feel oppressed by and (ineffectually) try to appropriate. The gun is also endowed with a purely cinematic mystique – the boys on the rooftop discuss it in terms of Mel Gibson's *Lethal Weapon* series[10] – and it is, clearly, symbolic in gender terms. For the moment, however, I am more concerned with how it functions structurally. The gun is a classic motivating device: being lost, it has to be found, and then it has to be used. Vinz announces that he will 'waste a cop' in sequence 5. He proves unable to do so, but Hubert will carry out the deed on his behalf. The gun structures the film by reappearing at regular intervals: in the tunnel, at Astérix's, with the skinheads, in the fantasy killing of the traffic wardens, in the final shoot-out. Throughout, it reinforces Vinz's centrality as well as the iconic power of the gun: the recurring image of Vinz brandishing it has become an emblem of the film.

In *La Haine*, people tell stories that are in themselves significant but that also constitute a structuring device. The stories form part of the quiet/crisis pattern of the film, which we have already mentioned, occurring principally in sequences 2 (Saïd tells Vinz a joke about 'killing for nothing'), 4 (a young *Beur* tells a story about candid camera), 10 (the old man in the toilets) and 15 (Hubert to Vinz about 'society falling'). The latter is the most important structurally, a framing story that opens and closes the film. On the soundtrack Hubert's voice talks of 'a man who falls from the 50th floor of a building and keeps saying: "So far so good…so far so good" – what matters is not the fall but the landing'. At the end, the word 'man' is replaced by 'society'. As he tells the story to Vinz on the rooftop, the latter says he knows the same story but with a rabbi – a joke on Vinz (whose automatic retort to any story this seems to be) but also a way to point out that it is the structure of the story as much as its contents which counts. It may also serve as a cinephilic reference to *The Magnificent Seven* (John Sturges, 1960), in which a similar story is told. This framing story has prompted interestingly split responses. Many commentators have argued that *La Haine* is 'about' the ending, the tragedy of violence in the *cités*; Kassovitz claims, 'I knew the ending before I knew the storyline. Everything is about the end, the last five seconds.'[11] But it is also the case that, as critic Roger Ebert perceptively noted, 'The film is not about its ending. It is not about the landing, but about the fall.'[12] We can see a *mise en abyme*[13] of this emphasis on *process* rather than ending within the

The revelation

Vinz admires it

Fooling around

Astérix

Vinz and his 'fake gun'

Threatening the skinhead

Notre-Dame triumphs

The gun as structuring device

The Mexican stand-off

film, as it is the telling and the listening to stories that is the point rather than their contents. In fact, crucial elements are often missing, such as the name of the central character in the candid camera story. The 'ending' of the framing story is the link between the film and the social issue it addresses; but the 'fall', the process of telling the story, is the possibility of making artistic meaning out of it; in other words, it signifies the film itself.

Virtuoso noir: the aesthetics of *La Haine*

The opening sequence

La Haine begins with a grainy image of a young man, seen from the back, facing a line of police and shouting at them: 'You are nothing but assassins. It is easy for you, you have weapons. We only have stones' (as he throws one). His looks and accent immediately establish him as from the *banlieue*. The images – possibly shot for the film, since there is synchronised sound – are extremely grainy. There is no music. There follows a black screen with the beginning of the credits, and then a man's voice (Hubert's) telling a story about a man falling from a 50-floor building, over a terrestrial globe that bursts into flames as a home-made 'bomb' (in a bottle) is thrown at it. These images were initially in colour, but they are now in black and white, both on the DVD and the print re-released in 2004 (more on this later). In those few seconds several themes are planted: the uneven confrontation between young people and the police, violence and the *banlieue*, and the notion that this situation is (a) global and (b) will lead to an 'explosion' – in a nugget, the 'message' of the film. Immediately afterwards, a montage of newsreel images begins, over which the credits are superimposed. On the soundtrack we can now hear Bob Marley's 'Burnin' and Lootin'', a song that is as cool in musical style as it is political in its lyrics. Marley asks, 'How many rivers do we have to cross, Before we can talk to the boss', and warns that 'We gonna be…burnin' and a-lootin' tonight', referring to the police as 'uniforms of brutality'.

This opening sequence lasts altogether five minutes and nine seconds. For it, Kassovitz watched dozens of hours of material,[14] mainly composed of newsreel footage of events over the ten years leading to the making of *La Haine*. The sequence, on first viewing, appears as a blur of images of police and young demonstrators, moving extremely rapidly: the average shot length is just over four seconds, even though some of the footage has been slowed down. Looking more closely, there is, however, a clear structure and progression to the montage, which can be roughly divided into three sections.

The first section alternates shots of CRS police and young people (reminiscent of the student riots of May 1968, in particular with a close-up of a CRS bludgeon). It contrasts the serried ranks of police uniforms against the softer shapes of the students, whose actions begin with quiet marching and dancing but end in looting (possibly of a bank), directly echoing Marley's words on the soundtrack. Section two moves on to individual violence, evoking in particular Malik Oussekine and Makome M'Bowole (two victims of police violence) with images of the demonstrations that followed their deaths, more explicitly in the case of Oussekine: we see the entry code of the building where he was fatally beaten, and his body which medics are trying to revive. A poster says 'Don't forget the police kills' and 'CRS = SS' (a favourite May 1968 slogan), and graffiti ask that 'justice be done for Makome'. The two deaths, seven years apart, are merged into one by the relative anonymity of the images[15] and their rapid flow.

Whereas sections one and two contain images of Paris shot during the day, the third section moves to the night-time *banlieue*, starting with the burning of a shopping mall. Young people's violence is more extreme, suggesting (perhaps subliminally) retaliation for police violence in the preceding sections and/or that the *banlieue* is intrinsically more dangerous than the city centre. Though the geographical order is reversed (Paris, then the *banlieue*), the temporal shift from day to night prefigures the film to come. About one-third through this last section, the sound level of the Marley song decreases and diegetic noises begin to be heard (young people shouting, breaking glass, thuds). Then, towards the end, the voice-over of a television presenter commenting on the riots can be heard. The section ends with the television presenter talking to camera, and, finally, a picture of Abdel, reportedly in a coma in hospital. The montage we have just seen is identified as 'television' when it is 'switched off' and fades to a white spot before the film proper begins.

This opening montage is not simply a 'documentary' thematically preparing us for the fiction to come; in structure and progression it contains the shape of the film to come: towards greater violence, from day to night, and a contrast between city and *banlieue*. In a more subtle way the opening blurs the boundary between 'reality' and 'fiction', in image and sound: Marley fades slightly to give way to diegetic sounds and the voice of the presenter, but it then bridges the gap into the fictional opening, over which it will be faintly heard, for a short while. The move from montage to fiction also creates a contrast between the grainy, 'dirty' and blurred figures of riots at night, and the sharp, elegant black and white daytime pictures, as we switch from 'television' to 'film'.

Black and white in the age of colour

Making a black and white film in 1995 is a statement. Since colour became ubiquitous in the 1970s, a few filmmakers have continued to make black and white films. Famous examples include Woody Allen (*Manhattan*, 1979; *Celebrity*, 1998), Spike Lee (*She's Gotta Have It*, 1986) and Martin Scorsese (*Raging Bull*, 1980). Various justifications have been put forward for this choice. In the case of *Raging Bull*, it has been argued by Scorsese that black and white makes the blood less disturbing and that, technically, it fades less than colour.[16] Black and white also gives a period feel to a film set in the 1940s and 1950s.

Insofar as colour contributes, in V.F. Perkins' words, to 'an ideal conception of a cinema complete with natural sound and colour',[17] then black and white (today) appears particularly non-realistic. In fact, such is the perceived distance between naturalism and black and white that the Dogme movement, perhaps *the* index of naturalism in contemporary cinema, 'banned' it. Rule 4 of the Dogme manifesto (which, incidentally, appeared the same year as *La Haine*) states that 'the film must be in colour'; black and white is 'an indulgence'.[18] Black and white could be considered such an 'indulgence' for *La Haine*; it certainly gives the film a superficial resemblance to 'cool' music videos. It also confers an aura of cinephilic homage, for instance to *Raging Bull* and *She's Gotta Have It*, two films Kassovitz particularly admired. As in these two films, black and white also allows for a more overt play on the heroes' skin colours and in particular Hubert's. The first time we see him, boxing, his naked torso and face have clearly been oiled to reflect light – a common practice to overcome the 'problem' of black skin's lesser refraction of light, as discussed by Richard Dyer.[19] In the range of stylistic references afforded by the use of black and white, film noir is also drawn upon, in particular in the sequences where Vinz goes to the cinema and the boxing match. These make use of classic noir photography, with *chiaroscuro* and backlighting – for instance in the cinema scene with its baroque smoke patterns. The scene of Vinz and his friends in the BMW shows him looking moodily at the street, streetlights reflecting in the car window. In these moments, black and white constructs a noir mood of urban edginess and expectancy. The fact that these are all focused on Vinz confirms his privileged status. Another function of black and white is to distinguish *La Haine* from the other *banlieue* and *beur* films (which are virtually all in colour)[20] as well as from television reportage – indeed, it is interesting how 'ordinary' the colour scenes that have been cut out of *La Haine*[21] look by contrast with the film we know. Using black and white enables Kassovitz, on a relatively

Noir on black: light reflecting on Hubert

Moody urban photography: Vinz and Santo in the
BMW

Noir lighting: Vinz smoking in the cinema

modest budget, to make the architecture of the *cité* 'very beautiful [and] graphic'.[22]

And yet black and white in *La Haine* also retains the value of realism because of its link with genres connoted as realistic (newsreels, archival footage, *cinéma vérité*, neo-realism, the new wave), especially so as the film has a clear social angle. Ultimately, the brilliance of *La Haine* is that it draws equally on the realist and anti-naturalist connotations of black and white, making the film appear both 'gritty' and 'cool', drawing us into the topic and at the same time giving us an aesthetic distance from it.

Camerawork

Together with the use of black and white the most striking features of *La Haine*'s *mise en scène* are the mobility of the camera combined with the use of long takes, and some self-conscious, flashy effects. There are several remarkable *plans-séquences* – defined as a 'long take articulated to represent the equivalent of a sequence' (in the sense of a succession of events)[23] – especially in the first half of the film, particularly noticeable in black and white and wide-screen (the film's ratio is 1:85:1), producing strong horizontal and diagonal compositions and a sophisticated play on the gaze.

La Haine is made of (by my count) 352 shots. For a total length of 87 minutes, this gives – excluding the montage sequence – an average shot length (ASL) of almost 15 seconds (14.95 to be exact – 13.75 if one includes the montage). If this is not unusual for a French film, it is remarkably slow compared to American movies, whose ASL in the 1990s, according to David Bordwell, typically averaged between three and six seconds.[24] The average figure of 15 seconds, however, disguises huge differences: *La Haine* alternates long takes lasting 40 seconds or more (some more than one minute) with clusters of very short ones. For instance, action scenes use very rapid cutting: the exchange between the three boys and the television journalists (38 seconds in nine takes: ASL 4.2 seconds), the car theft (two minutes 22 seconds for 24 takes: ASL 5.9 seconds) and Vinz's imaginary shooting of the traffic wardens (28 seconds for 14 takes: ASL 2 seconds).

A lot has been made, including by Kassovitz, of the different ways of shooting the *cité* in the first half of the film as opposed to Paris in the second half: 'The idea – though it's hard to bring off – was that on the estate we should use short lenses, to fix people against the background, and then much longer lenses in Paris, to detach them and really have them stand out.'[25] Kassovitz also asked director of photography Pierre Aïm to make sure 'that the Paris shots should be more grainy'.[26] One reason why the different treatment is less noticeable than Kassovitz wished is that there are more indoor scenes in Paris and they virtually all take place at night. The graininess therefore seems 'natural', and the relationship between the characters and the wider spaces is both less developed and less visible than in the *cité*. More noticeable is the larger proportion of long mobile takes in the first half: in the *cité* section there are 18 shots of more than 45 seconds, against eight in the second, and, strikingly, ten shots of over one minute in the first half against only one in the second half. Some of these qualify as *plans-séquences*. These kinds of shots are normally considered difficult to shoot and therefore evidence of skill. Kassovitz has – not very convincingly – claimed he likes doing them because he is 'lazy'[27] and does not like editing. A more likely reason is that, as he also says, he likes 'actors to be in the same shot'.[28] Indeed, in the most remarkable *plan-séquence* of the film, in which we follow the three heroes walking though the *cité*, 'the actors' performances must adapt to this very precise mechanism'.[29] The trick is to make this 'precise mechanism' appear 'natural'.

Let us examine this *plan-séquence* in detail. It is the most extreme in both length (one minute 54 seconds) and spatial span. It is also a key shot in its articulation of the heroes' relationship to the *cité*. The camera (on Steadycam) starts from behind three policemen walking towards Vinz, Saïd and Hubert. The similarity in numbers highlights the differences: to the uniformity and anonymity of the cops (whose faces we don't see) the camera contrasts the diversity of the three friends. The choreography of people and camera at this point offers a *mise en abyme* of the film, illustrating the dynamic confrontation between youth and police. The camera then 'loses' the cops and picks up the three friends, following them between two buildings. As they reach a small square they pause, trying to identify the noise of a motorbike, while the camera circles round them in medium close-up. The identification of the noise points to their aural familiarity with their environment. They start walking again, talking about a woman; they pass a group of young blacks and *Beurs,* who greet Vinz – demonstrating again their familiarity with the *cité* and its racial hybridity. We move on again to a more open space, where Hubert detaches himself from the group to meet a young *Beur* whom he sells drugs to. The neatness of this pause – a trifle facile, perhaps – is in the echo between Hubert and the young man touching hands in the foreground (exchanging drugs for money) and a mural in the background reproducing the famous image of two hands meeting from Michelangelo's Sistine Chapel. The friends gather again and move into a building.

The next scene, which follows the three boys on the roof of the block, is composed of 11 shots, including three over one minute long. As in the *plan-séquence* analysed above, the long and fluid takes that follow our heroes

Three moments in the *plan-séquence* in the *cité*

among a gathering already in full swing (with music and barbecue), impart to the spectator the energy of youth and the dynamism of the relationships. The young people's mastery of space, symbolised by the elevated position and the expanses visible from the rooftop, is short-lived (the gathering is interrupted by the police) but it is real. By contrast, in Paris the camera shows them dwarfed by architecture (for instance, in the empty Gare Saint-Lazare) or boxed in, as in the art gallery or the police station, as if to emphasise their 'out-of-place-ness' and lack of prospects in the metropolis.

Two other noticeable sets of long takes are those that depict Vinz and Hubert at home. The scene in Vinz's home (sequence 2) is dealt with in just three long takes: one around his bedroom (46 seconds) one with the rest of the family (35 seconds), and one of him talking to himself in the mirror (31 seconds). Similarly, Hubert's home environment in sequence 7 is dealt with in just two long takes: the first one follows him through the flat into the kitchen with his mother (one minute three seconds) and the second one around the dining table (one minute three seconds). In both cases, the length and mobility of the takes establish a relationship between characters and environment, both the chaotic warmth of Vinz's home and the relative calm in Hubert's.

The virtuoso aspect of the camerawork, especially in the first half of the film, is enhanced by flamboyant effects, which contribute to the youthful, dynamic image of the film and are testament to Kassovitz's precocious talent. These effects fall into five categories.

(1) Mirrors and confined locations

The most notorious mirror moment in *La Haine* is a trick. The scene in which Vinz, in front of his bathroom mirror, imitates Robert De Niro in *Taxi Driver* was shot... without a mirror, with an extra standing in for Vinz's back, in order to avoid the problem of the camera reflecting in the mirror in such a small location.[30] As the camera approaches the 'mirror' the extra dips down, and we get close to Vinz supposedly looking into a mirror, but in reality looking straight at the camera. By contrast, the scene in which Vinz cuts Saïd's hair was done conventionally. The most remarkable use of mirrors is in the café toilet scene, where several mirrors reflecting on each other enlarge the visible space and produce a sense of disorientation. The screen is split by the divisions between mirrors, so that the boys seem isolated from each other while they are physically very close. One shot, which has the camera pointing at a mirror and then rapidly tracking to the 'real' characters, produces a particularly dizzying effect and an extended play on the gaze: the characters seem to be looking straight at the camera when they are not, or to be looking away from each other when in fact they are facing each other. This scene, like that of Vinz imitating De Niro, quite classically uses mirrors as a means of depicting a reflection on the self, in this case the heroes' shattered identity. It should be saluted, equally, as an illustration of Kassovitz and Aïm's skilful exploitation of confined locations and reflective surfaces.

(2) Editing juxtapositions

Incongruous or shocking images are inserted with no device indicating that they are 'fantasy' – for instance, the cow in the *cité* seen by Vinz and the spectator but not by Saïd, and Vinz dancing to Jewish music. Most disconcerting (on first viewing) is Vinz's 'shooting' of two traffic wardens in Les Halles. As with images of the gun, we note that these textual flourishes, apart from their purely spectacular value, privilege Vinz by building up his subjectivity.

(3) Striking camera positions

There are many of these, of which I will mention three. The first is the lateral tracking shot along the line of police cars that opens the film after the montage. The shot starts from Saïd's point of view, with the back of his head visible, then 'loses' him, then finds him again, surprisingly, at the end of the long line behind the police car. Thus, Saïd is both observer and participant, a position the film assigns to the spectator through him. Secondly, as Vinz and Hubert come down from Asterix's flat in sequence 11, the camera looks straight up the middle of the stairwell while rotating on itself, counter to the movement of the boys coming down, producing a dizzying effect. Finally, most noticeable (and famous) is the helicopter shot that accompanies the DJ's music over the *cité* in sequence 8. For this Kassovitz used a Belgian team specialised in shooting from low-flying aircraft, although it seems the shoot was difficult: 'There was too much wind and the blokes could not control the machine. We did it three times, we got insulted but we got there in the end.'[31] Other accounts suggest that the shot was truncated, a supposition supported by the fact that the shot has been slightly slowed down (as can be seen by the gait of the passers-by below) and yet is 'only' 46 seconds. Either way, the shot produces a strange, oneiric effect, giving the impression that we are floating unsteadily over the *cité*, like the DJ's music.

(4) 'In-camera' tricks

This most memorable of these is the 'compressed zoom' on the three heroes as they arrive in Paris (standing on Montparnasse station terrace – here

Kassovitz played with verisimilitude, since their trains in reality arrive at Saint-Lazare, as we see when later they try and catch it). This type of shot has a long lineage, from Hitchcock's 1958 *Vertigo*, where it expresses the protagonist's (James Stewart) mental dislocation; here it suggests the boys are 'out of place' in the city centre, particularly so as the street behind them, Rue de Rennes, leads to Saint-Germain-des-Prés, the heart of bourgeois-bohemian Paris. Also remarkable is the scene outside the nightclub, which shows Vinz's face in close-up on the left and the (fantasy) killing of the club bouncer in long shot on the right. This was filmed in a single shot but the effect, obtained with contrasted lighting,[32] suggests two different spaces in the frame and thus hints – again – at Vinz's mental disorder.

(5) Tricks done through processing

La Haine is punctuated by a series of 'white flashes', in which a brief whitening of the screen is accompanied by a violent, swishing sound. This occurs, for example, in the garage, as Vinz reveals the hidden gun, and when the BMW slams into reverse in sequence 13. In the garage scene the image is also speeded up, accompanied by a bullet-like noise. The impact of these

Vinz imagines the killing outside the night-club

sound/image effects is to generate a sense of speed, of energy, as well as giving the impression of 'magic'.

On occasion, the combination of fluid camerawork, striking compositions and flashy, 'mannerist' effects recall the *cinéma du look* of Jean-Jacques Beineix (for instance, *Diva*, 1981) and Luc Besson (*Nikita*, 1990). If at times we can agree with Kassovitz that 'it's all too much, almost complacent, like a music video',[33] on the whole the effects are well integrated into the rest of the *mise en scène*. In this way, *La Haine* presents its socially oriented story of 'ordinary' young men in non-glamorous *banlieue* surroundings, but makes them and their decor exciting. For example, the helicopter shot gives us an aesthetically pleasing, yet 'documentary', view of the *cité*, while the unusual shape of the buildings is more visible without the distraction of colour. Kassovitz also makes the decor 'speak'. During the 'candid camera' joke (sequence 4), the walls behind the characters are sprayed with tags saying 'force' and 'energy', when the characters are particularly listless; in the garage there is a tag saying 'La haine' behind Vinz as he pulls the gun out. By providing a visceral, oral and visual excitement such devices contributed to the success of the film, and outside France they helped compensate for the 'handicap' of a foreign-language soundtrack – especially for a young audience with low tolerance for subtitles. In this respect, the film's use of sound and music was also crucial.

Sound and music

The two halves of the film are split orally, just as they are visually: 'The estate is done in stereo, with broad sound, whereas Paris is all in mono. Unfortunately, that doesn't really come across.'[34] Kassovitz is right, although there is undoubtedly a greater density of sounds in the *cité*, where layers of voices, noises and faint music in the background richly surround the dialogues. The aim was clearly to produce a naturalistic ambience: 'We used city sounds which became a music of our own – a growl, a layer of sound but a natural layer.'[35] At the same time, sound is also used in an expressionist manner, where the nature of the sounds and their amplification (trains hissing, cars howling, gun shots resonating or swishing past) contribute to the climate of violence.

Contrary to what most first-time viewers remember, there is surprisingly little music in *La Haine*; so little, in fact, that the CD of the soundtrack is half made up of music from *Métisse*. But the power of association with music, especially rap music, is such that several critics 'heard' a lot of hip-hop music in the film. Olivier Mongin (whose analysis is otherwise often pertinent) even quotes lyrics from several rap songs 'which punctuate the film',[36] whereas they are not in the film but can be found on the CD of rap music 'inspired' by *La Haine* (see Chapter 3). There are, in fact, only six moments in the film when music is more than a background, and all, apart from the opening Bob Marley song, are brief or very brief. They are as follows (further details can be found on the credits in Appendix 1):

1. The credits ('Burnin' and Lootin'', sung by Bob Marley)
2. Vinz's Jewish dance (wedding song medley)
3. Hubert smoking ('That Loving Feeling', sung by Isaac Hayes)
4. The DJ sequence (sampling of rap/funk music and Edith Piaf's 'Je ne regrette rien')
5. Break-dancing ('Outstanding', sung by The Gap Band)
6. Music in the BMW ('Mon esprit part en couilles', sung by Expression Direkt)

   La Haine eschews the contemporary tendency for ubiquitous music on the soundtrack. It also avoids the classic use of film music as emotional enhancement. Kassovitz said, 'The editor would try to lay on great layers, which always seemed to work. He tried the music from *Léon* [Luc Besson, 1994] at the end. It's incredible, you can't help crying. I don't like that.'[37] Music does however, play the important function of cultural identification in a number of ways. All but the last number listed above are heard in the *cité*, firmly connecting it to a specific kind of music. The number featured in Paris, 'Mon esprit part en couilles', is heard in the BMW, with the boys from the *cité* singing along, stressing their organic relation to it, as if they were transporting it with them (in addition, one of the actors in the car, Solo Dicko, is a rap singer). A self-confessed lover of hip-hop, Kassovitz claims that, while making *La Haine*, 'all the time I thought of rhythm and this comes from rap'.[38] Yet rap is far from dominant and the soundtrack also includes reggae, disco-inspired soul, funk, R&B, Arabic music and snippets of French chanson (Edith Piaf).[39] This medley – which I suspect reflects Kassovitz's personal taste rather than a plausible version of the characters' music favourites – is culturally hybrid, American-dominated (no French pop) and youth-oriented (no jazz). The faint echoes of Schubert's 'Ave Maria' at Asterix's are clearly ironic, a marker of an alien high culture that is, like Asterix's flat, borrowed. The other key point is that the music is racially mixed, in line with the ideological project of the film. It provides an ethnic rallying point rather than a divisive one, unlike, for instance, *Do The Right Thing*, in which Italian crooners clash violently with African-American music. In this respect the film rather resembles *Hangin' With the Homeboys*, where African-American and Latino music happily mix on the soundtrack, like the protagonists.

   Thus, music in *La Haine* establishes a cultural climate, an ambience that suggests a harmonious ethnic blend, social concern and love of American and American-inspired music. It also, on three occasions, evokes a utopian space: Marley's song on the opening montage, despite its belligerent lyrics, has an elegiac quality; Hubert's dope-smoking scene over soul music is marked by the continuity of music and time passing, signalled by fades; the break-dancing sequence smoothly edits the various dancers over one funky song. All three moments suggest, albeit briefly, the utopian space of the classical musical film, which is in each case brutally interrupted: the sound of a gunshot at the end of the montage, Hubert being called out, a boy bursting into the break-dancing arena with the news that violence has erupted in the *cité*. In the latter, in particular, the 'reality' of the dystopian French *banlieue* has invaded the semi-oneiric space conjured up by the 'foreign' music. The camera, however, stays in the dream-like, musical space, pointing at the spinning dancer while everyone else decamps, as if it wanted to remain for a moment longer in the utopian 'American' space.

Vinz, Saïd, Hubert: an explosive trio

Looks and performances

A crucial factor in the appeal of *La Haine* is its central trio of protagonists, with whom the film creates strong empathy. Vinz, Saïd, and Hubert are onscreen virtually all the time, strongly contributing to the youth appeal of the film. The trio of young men are part heroes, part villains, all at once social victims, attractive and sympathetic survivors and 'little jerks'.[40] Constantly bickering, they are nevertheless inseparable; similarly, despite their contrasting skin colour and religious signs (a Muslim Fatma's hand for Saïd, a Jewish Star of David for Vinz, a Catholic cross for Hubert), their shared habitat, clothing and language reinforce their common identity as *banlieue* boys. The naturalistic performance of the three charismatic young actors, whose first names are also those of the characters, contributes substantially to the film's aura of authenticity.

Vinz – the aggressive one

Vincent Cassel, who plays Vinz, was the most experienced actor of the trio at the time, and he subsequently became a star, something that inevitably affects subsequent viewings. But, even without this knowledge, Vinz attracts most attention as the most full-fledged character, whose incongruous or violent fantasies (a cow in the middle of the *cité*, Jewish dancing, shootings) we have privileged access to.

Vinz is all about aggression, as signalled by the first shot of him, featuring the chunky knuckleduster bearing his name, as if he was thrusting his fist at the spectator's face, even in his sleep. Cassel's long, sharp face is accentuated by his closely shaved head, skinhead-style, for which the director had to twist the actor's arm: 'Vincent said, "I'll look awful." [...] He knows his ears stick out.'[41] His facial expressions delineate the look further: hostile stare, menacing grimaces underlined by thin lips, spitting, grinding teeth. His speech is a mixture of aggression and inarticulacy, suggesting suppressed hatred about to erupt: his occasional stutter makes words even more explosive when they emerge. Cassel uses his tall and lanky body in a highly kinetic fashion, thanks to his ballet training (the Jewish dance was his idea). He projects aggression with threatening arm movements and uncouth gestures, such as picking his nose or squeezing his blackheads (likewise, the first image of him asleep shows him drooling). Cassel's talent consists in making this violent performance graceful as well.

Vinz's clothes complete this aggressive persona. He wears standard sports clothes – a Nike jacket and trainers – with jeans and a black leather blouson, updating the look of 1950s *blousons noirs* delinquents. His room, which contains photos of football players and of Bruce Lee, a large sound system and an impressive stack of trainers, continues the macho, sporty theme. There is a tin of hashish and a poster of a cannabis leaf, as well as a tidy desk and computer. Thus, the character is presented as a 'normal' adolescent with just a hint of rebellion. Olivier Seguret's view that Vinz takes revenge on 'the absolute social denial in which he lives'[42] is contradicted by this bedroom and what we see of his aggressive but playful relationship to his family. Kassovitz's autobiographically driven depiction of a warm Jewish family to some extent clashes with, or at least complicates, the characterisation of a socially deprived hooligan.

Saïd the 'joker'

Saïd (Saïd Taghmaoui) is introduced by the graffiti he sprays on the police car, which proudly states his name and says 'fuck the police'. His handsome, chiselled face, sallow complexion and short, dark curly hair – as well as the Fatma's hand pendant – signal him as a *Beur*. Unlike Vinz and Hubert, however, his family environment remains off-screen. We briefly see his sister and his brother Nordine, and he refers to his parents, who would 'tear into him' if he took part in the riots, but we never enter his home. This absence has been controversial. Carrie Tarr believes the film thereby erases Maghrebi culture, while Myrto Konstantarakos argues that Saïd's absence of on-screen home is a positive step, as the film this way avoids singling out the otherness of *beur* culture.[43] As these diametrically opposed views show, this issue, in terms of ethnic inscription, is largely a matter of extra-textual interpretation. But the fact remains that Saïd as a character is denied one layer of depth granted to the others.

Similarly, while Vinz is associated with the gun and Hubert – initially – with boxing, Saïd lacks such a 'prop'. He is, however, distinguished by his sartorial flash and his gift of the gab. Saïd is clearly fashion-conscious, wearing a Sergio Tacchini tracksuit,[44] his leather blouson softened by a (presumably fake) fur collar. His woolly hat is a Lacoste, as is his brother's cardigan. These clothes are plausible, especially among *beur* and black *banlieue* youth, who have made brands such as Lacoste and Burberry into a cult. Saïd Taghmaoui's performance is also characterised by a lot of energetic movement, partly to make up for his small stature compared with his two tall friends, but unlike Vinz, his gesticulations – his swooping arm gestures in particular – are not aggressive. His attempts to assert his authority (for instance, over his sister and Astérix) end up more as tantrums or provocation, and he lies about women and sex – the film thereby tends to undermine his authority. Nevertheless, his gift for words, his *tchatche* (effusive volubility) and constant jokes are a large contribution to the film's inventiveness and pleasure. Saïd's relationship to language is signalled straightaway by his introductory graffiti, and he is the one who alters the 'Yours' (to '*Ours*') in the 'The World is Yours' poster with a spray can. His way of sending up learned culture, for instance the exaggeratedly precious tone he adopts to say 'on y vââ?' (shall we go?) in front of the art gallery, or 'merci, Châârles...' to the waiter, is typical of a certain kind of *banlieue* language, which defensively parodies learned French as both bourgeois and effeminate.[45] In this respect, one function of his character is to show language as the – ultimately ineffectual – weapon of the dispossessed.

Hubert 'the wise'

Everything about Hubert (Hubert Koundé) celebrates his blackness (as we saw in Chapter 1, this goes back to Kassovitz's first short, *Fierrot le pou,* and to his first feature, *Métisse,* the latter also co-starring Koundé). His hair is plaited in an Afro-American style and he first appears with his glistening naked torso on display, an image duplicated in the poster, which shows him in classic boxer posture. Later we see his bedroom replete with images of iconic black athletes, such as Muhammad Ali. In keeping with this introduction, he wears the most sports-oriented clothes, with a hint of the military: combat fatigues, an Everlast T-shirt (another reference to boxing) showing under a sweatshirt jacket and a hood, and Reebok trainers. The

Saïd's tag

Vinz's ring

Hubert's poster

introductory slow-motion boxing is a reference to the credits sequence of *Raging Bull* but it also emphasises control; boxing is a classic feature of American male-oriented genres, especially gangster films, where it serves to display and channel male power, competitive combat and controlled aggression. Accordingly, Hubert is all calm strength, without the chaotic aggression of Vinz or the overheated verbosity of Saïd. The devastation of his gym symbolises an attack on his identity and ambitions – subliminally signified by the *torn* poster that introduces him.

Compared to Saïd and Vinz, Hubert is all calm, cool and consideration. Koundé, who is very tall, seems to tower effortlessly over the others, dominating by presence alone. Although he ignores his sister, Hubert speaks gently to his mother (as opposed to Vinz, who shouts at his relatives) and discreetly supports the household. He is quiet and dignified, his speech containing noticeably fewer obscenities than the others. He repeatedly calms Vinz down, in the hospital, in the café toilet, in Les Halles. All the more paradoxical, then, that it is Hubert, the one most in control of his aggression, who chooses deliberately to use violence in the final shoot-out. After Vinz has surrendered his gun to him and is accidentally shot by Inspector Notre-Dame, Hubert thrusts his gun at the policeman's head. At this moment, Vinz's chaotic aggression gives way to Hubert's reasonable violence, justifying the use of the gun to avenge the police *bavures* against Abdel and now Vinz. 'Hate breeds hate,' Hubert says earlier. There is no mistaking the impact of the final scene: in this finality, we are made to accept violence as rational and inevitable.

Race and gender: black blanc beur ... *and macho*

Ethnic declension

In the reception of *La Haine* outside France, the issue of ethnicity has proved particularly controversial (see Chapter 3). On the one hand, the film's portrayal of *black blanc beur* harmony has been accused of whitewashing the reality of racism in France, while, on the other, the film is thought to promote a covert racist hierarchy – linked to the white identity of its director. It is thus worth looking at this thorny issue in some detail.

There is no doubting *La Haine*'s anti-racist intent, matching the director's well-known views. For Kassovitz, the brutal police interrogation of Saïd and Hubert in Paris is meant to convey 'how it was with Makome'.[46] In this scene, two policemen tower above and brutally manhandle the pair, who are tied to their chairs, while a trainee policeman looks on. Hubert and Saïd's possession of a little hashish is clearly out of proportion with the gratuitous police brutality, accompanied by a string of racist and sexist insults: as is traditional in French slang, feminised terms of abuse are used to degrade further their target.[47] Nude posters on the wall confirm the macho culture of the police. The young trainee's look at the scene, a mixture of fascination, revulsion and embarrassment, serves to underline both the institutional nature of this violence – he is 'learning' it – and the role of film and media: his gaze evidently duplicates ours. Later, the fight between the three friends and the skinheads reiterates the film's anti-racist stance, underlined by the skinheads' initial targeting of Saïd. Earlier, the same Saïd had also noted that 'an Arab in a police station does not last two hours', and later recounted an obscene, untranslatable and very funny joke about National Front leader Jean-Marie Le Pen. In putting these remarks in Saïd's mouth, the film articulates not just racism in France (and its opposition to it) but the awareness that *Beurs* are a special target of it.

Yet these instances of overt anti-racist discourse are relatively isolated. Moreover, despite the religious emblems around the heroes' necks, *La Haine* displays a complete lack of interest in religion: the only time the subject comes up, Vinz's grandmother berates him for no longer going to the synagogue. More strikingly, apart from a few affectionate jokes ('you bogus *Beur*', 'you poor Jew'), race plays no part in the heroes' relationship to each other and, instead, their friendship is repeatedly affirmed. The point of the racial diversity of the central trio is thus not racial conflict but racial cohesion, a key element in Kassovitz's depiction of urban warfare: 'I chose people of three different ethnic groups because I did not want to make a film about "Arabs against the police" or "blacks against the police", but about "young people from the *cités* against the police".'[48] This threesome ethnic declension could be seen as wishful thinking. Yet, in this respect, *La Haine* is close to the approach of many *beur* films, and to sociological accounts of racial relationships in the French *banlieue*, just as it differs from American films such as *Boyz 'N the Hood* and *Do The Right Thing*, where racial conflict drives the narrative. *Hangin' With the Homeboys*, as already mentioned, is an exception, since it also depicts a cohesive, ethnically mixed bunch of friends, although admittedly the group – made of Latinos and blacks – does not include whites. It is also possible to argue, along with Mireille Rosello, that 'black and white binary oppositions are slowly losing their status of obvious relevance. They are being displaced by more up-to-date representations of complex, hybrid, and multifaceted identities.'[49]

If ethnic difference is largely irrelevant among the inseparable trio of heroes, it is also because they are bound by class hatred for the 'establishment', or at least authority figures, whether police, the media, the bourgeois or a shopkeeper. Thus, the scene with the latter, although he is Vietnamese, is one of simple delinquency, unlike the similar episode in *Do The Right Thing*: Vinz tries to pay less for his grandmother's peppers while Saïd steals biscuits. Furthermore, while, as we have seen, some of the police brutality towards Hubert and Saïd is racist, the police force is itself ethnically mixed. The friendly *beur* community cop Samir (Karim Belkhadra) is not the only non-white policeman; his colleagues at the hospital and in the devastated police station in the *cité* include *beur* and black members. More conspicuously, one of the two policemen who maltreat Saïd and Hubert in Paris is a *Beur*, played by well-known *beur* actor Zinedine Soualem. *La Haine* contrives to showcase the extra brutality against the non-white characters by having Vinz come out of the building later and run faster than the policeman after him, but overall the message is clear: while there is racism in the police, its violence is institutional rather than racial. *La Haine* does not ignore racism, but it adopts a non-Manichean, non-essentialist approach to ethnic difference.

To take the point further, yet, can we agree with Carrie Tarr[50] that *La Haine*, despite its good intentions, reinforces a racist agenda, by putting the white character first and marginalising *beur* identity most? Looking closely at the film text, it appears that Vinz does not actually feature in significantly more shots than his comrades but that he is the object of many more close-ups. As we saw above, he is also given a richer, more rounded characterisation than the other two.[51] The gun, which he shows off at frequent intervals, makes him more prominent in visual compositions as well as in the publicity for the film. Thus, Vinz is privileged on a visual, narrative and iconic level. By contrast, although Saïd's irony and humour make a large contribution to spectatorial pleasure, he is less assertive a presence in the film. His gaze opens the film and he is the survivor at the end, but this does not grant him narrative authority and it is at the price of his marginalisation from the main action. More insidiously, Hubert is celebrated according to fashionable cultural criteria but denied social progress. His advocacy of non-violence and desire to escape poverty through boxing come to nothing in the climactic ending. He may, in the final violent blast we don't see, also be its victim, but the fact remains that he uses the gun of his own accord, while Inspector Notre-Dame shoots Vinz by mistake. This finale, while justifying *banlieue* violence, can also be seen to reinforce – unwittingly – racist stereotypes, showing the white character as victim of police violence (although he is the most violent himself), the *Beur* as impotent witness and the black not only linked to drug trafficking but also the perpetrator of violence.

Summing up the points about ethnic declension, we see a number of paradoxes. *La Haine* exposes examples of racism, especially (though not exclusively) on the part of white characters, but it privileges its white leading character. The film worships aspects of blackness (looks, music) and portrays its black hero as the most dignified, yet it also aligns him with drug dealing and deliberate – as opposed to blundering – violence. Racism against *Beurs* is pointed up as the most virulent, yet one of the perpetrating policemen is himself a *Beur,* and out of the three leads Saïd is, in narrative terms, the most marginalised. It would be reductive to consider these features as de facto 'racist'. At best the film is confused, at worst it is politically naive – as, for instance, when Vinz in the café toilet compares himself to *beur* victim Malik Oussekine. But these confusions themselves derive from the inherent complexity of the real-life situation. Anyone travelling the French suburbs can see plenty of evidence of ethnically mixed groups of young people, yet there is no denying the racism in the same areas, or in France in general.

Some of this complexity is in evidence in the inclusion of Jewishness, which, as Mireille Rosello points out, 'continues to remain an elusive signifier in French cultures'.[52] This may be why Vinz's Jewishness has been given short shrift: he tends to be simply seen as 'white'. If, as discussed in Chapter 1, there is an element of self-indulgence in the inclusion of Jewish folklore, it is also possible to follow Kassovitz in seeing a greater purpose to it. The old man's story about Siberia, which evokes the Holocaust, takes place at the centre of the film and it visibly troubles the three protagonists. As directorial intervention it raises the film's awareness of racism to another level of reflection, and most spectators understand Kassovitz's intention: 'This scene asks the question of how far you can go with hatred, Nazi hatred. Because the ghettos were not like Saint-Denis, they were much worse.'[53] The story also shares a crucial similarity with the framing story about the 'fall' and the film itself, in that it has a tragic finality: death.

If, however clumsily, *La Haine* attempts to depict ethnic difference in the deprived *cités* with some complexity, the same cannot be said of its representation of gender.

An infantile macho world

La Haine is clearly a youth-oriented film, centred on three quasi-adolescent men. Moreover, the absence of male authority figures, in common with many *banlieue* and *beur* films, is striking. The few older men who appear – Saïd's older brother Nordine, *beur* local cop Samir, the drunk who helps them in their attempt to steal the car – are all ineffectual. As Roy Stafford points out, apart from the old man in the café toilets, 'there is no parental/patriarchal figure who tells the youths how to behave'.[54] Heads of families are female: aunts, mothers, grandmothers. Similarly, society's representatives are female (the television newscaster, the journalist). Yet this does not mean that the heroes thereby occupy the place of the absent father. They live at home in a state of perpetual adolescence and their cultural discussions are confined to children's cartoons. None of them can drive so the attempted car theft is doomed to failure, an image of their lack of potency. When Saïd tells a story about having wild sex with a woman, the others' instant derision shows it to be fantasy. His story is, significantly, told in a playground, under a giant hippopotamus statue, which dwarfs and seems to mock them. Their disastrous encounter with women in the art gallery is about sexual as much as social ineptitude. In the light of this it is difficult to agree with Olivier Mongin that Saïd is involved in the world of male prostitution through the ambivalent figure of Astérix.[55]

Yet, at the same time, our heroes inhabit a testosterone-fuelled world of boxing, obscene language and gun-toting violence: their favourite insult is 'nique ta mère' (literally, 'fuck your mother'); the rap song in the car is the aggressively macho 'Mon esprit part en couille' by Expression Direkt; Vinz's shaved head and leather jacket, Hubert's fatigues, all connote a macho world validated by the film. The sequence of events around Vinz going to the cinema and the boxing match, as well as the police station scene, make a strong statement about a violent male culture that reproduces itself. The films Vinz sees in the cinema are all violent – among them a Clint Eastwood movie – and, pointedly, a child admiringly imitates his gesture in which his hand becomes a pretend gun, like the trainee cop watching to learn his 'trade'. Like the macho obscenities, it could be argued that the masculinist stance of the three heroes is just that (a posture, which comes to nothing; despite his bravado and imitation of De Niro in *Taxi Driver*, Vinz is incapable of firing a gun), or even that the film offers a critique of this macho world. This point, however, would have more critical force if the film itself did not derive most of its spectacle, and thus pleasure, from images of macho violence. And, as I showed earlier, the most beautiful noir photography showcases Vinz and his gun.

Reinforcing this is the absence of female characters capable of providing a critical perspective on the misogynist obscenities. Women are barely glimpsed at home, cooking, sewing and doing homework. On the rare occasions that they appear in public (Saïd's sister, the women at the art gallery), they are targets for crude aggression and unprovoked macho insults: 'squealer', 'cow', 'fish', 'Wonderbra advert', 'whore'. In this respect, *La Haine* does not simply reproduce the male focus and misogyny of most *beur* and *banlieue* films; it goes further – so much so that even French reviewers noticed. When tackled, Kassovitz has invariably replied with the debatable assertion that his film corresponds to the reality of the *banlieue*, where 'you don't mix genders'.[56] Women's perennial association with sexuality supposedly detracts from the seriousness of the film's purpose: 'I did not want to soften the topic: what would love have to do with this story?'[57] It does not seem to occur to Kassovitz that women have a social identity too: 'Maybe the film lacks a scene with girls among themselves... but that would have been another digression.'[58] Thus, women in *La Haine* are denied subjectivity (none of them qualifies as a character), their relation to the males is purely biological,[59] and they do not participate in social issues. It is thus surprising that Elisabeth Mahoney, after indicting films such as *Falling Down* and *Night on Earth* for their 'reliance on stereotypes of gender and race' despite their 'reconfiguration of urban space', praises *La Haine* for 'represent[ing] the possibility of reclaiming or re-imagining the space of the city',[60] but ignores its misogyny. The young men's behaviour and experience are presented as coterminous with the *banlieue*, with as a result, the impoverishment of its social depth, as we will see below.

Image and ideology in *La Haine*

'Social space'

In answer to a question about whether he had a purely visual attraction to the *banlieue*, Mathieu Kassovitz replied, 'No... it is more interesting to film because of the story. I prefer to speak of people in trouble rather than left-wing intellectuals in St-Germain-des-Prés.'[61] Having looked at issues of ethnicity and gender, this section asks what kind of social portrayal *La Haine* offers of 'people in trouble' in the *banlieue*.

We saw in Chapter 1 how films and television programmes about the *banlieue* repeatedly converge on a narrow scenario of male youth violence and delinquency, and on a visual vocabulary structured by a contrast between cramped and dark spaces (cluttered apartments, staircases, cellars and tunnels) and anonymous, empty spaces, a no man's land between the buildings. In contrast with other *banlieue* films, the design of Chanteloup-les-Vignes allows Kassovitz to eschew the straight lines and forbidding heights of brutal 1960s blocks. The dominant visual motif in *La Haine* is that of small, curved blocks with distinctive, 'vernacular' roof designs, children's playgrounds and small squares planted with trees. There are relatively few large, empty spaces. Two exceptions are what looks like an empty car park in front of the building in which Hubert's destroyed gym is situated (sequence 2) and the space in front of the three friends as they sit listening to a young boy's story (sequence 4). We also saw, earlier in this chapter, how the outdoor scenes in the *cité* are characterised by fluid camerawork and long takes, which establish a dynamic interaction between the characters and their environment. *La Haine* thus avoids the alienating look of many *banlieue* films and depicts a more integrated space on a more 'human' scale – see, for instance, the analysis of the *plan-séquence* earlier in this chapter.

On the other hand, compared not just to other *beur* films such as *Le Thé au harem d'Archimède*, *Hexagone* and *Raï* but also to American films depicting similar milieux, such as *Do The Right Thing* and *Clockers*, *La Haine* lacks what I would call 'social depth'. Unlike many other *banlieue* films with establishing shots that depict the borders between their *cité* and the rest of the world, *La Haine* never shows us how the *cité* stands in relation to its environment. It presents a self-enclosed world, in which the relentless focus on young men means that few spaces of social interaction are presented to the viewer. Largely because of the all-male focus, the views of 'normal' domestic spaces in Vinz and Hubert's homes are extremely brief (less than four minutes altogether), and, unlike in *beur* films – but also unlike in, say, *Mean Streets* – the three heroes never meet in cafés, restaurants or discos. Even the job centre, which recurs in so many *beur* and *banlieue* films, is absent. They do not belong to a school, gang or workplace; just about the only representation of 'employment' is small-scale dealing in drugs by Hubert and stolen goods (Darty,[62] the fence). The heroes of *La Haine* thus exist in a social vacuum where there are no possibilities of exchange or encounters.

Nor is *La Haine* a film 'about' delinquency or drugs in any conventional sense. Kassovitz claims he wanted to show the smoking of hashish, because 'in the street they smoke a lot and this is never shown in French cinema'.[63] Yet he spends little time on the question. There is a brief shot of Hubert smoking and of syringes on the ground (sequence 4) but the film does not chart the effects of drug taking, detrimental or otherwise – unlike, for instance, its contemporary, *Trainspotting*. More surprisingly, *La Haine's* treatment of violence is not as extensive as one might think. A comparison with *Clockers*, Spike Lee's story of exclusion and violence among young black males in a Brooklyn housing estate, is illuminating in this respect. Shocking images of blood and torn bodies graphically depict the *effect* of violence on the community: local people look aghast at the bodies. *La Haine*, on the other hand starts with political struggle in the opening montage. But these images are coded as historical. The ending is shocking in its *suggestion* of violence rather than its graphic depiction, since it leaves most of it off-screen. Similarly, one might say that *La Haine* is not 'about' the police in the way suggested by Kassovitz's insistence in interviews on the Makome *bavure* (see Chapter 1) and on his film countering police films such as *L627*. Contrary to the common perception of *La Haine* as a trenchant exposé of *banlieue* life, the social issues in the film are hinted at rather than explored.

It has been argued, with justification, that this lack of social depth is designed precisely to show the social vacuum in which the heroes live. For Mongin, *La Haine* situates its heroes in a space 'beyond any possible identity, whether it be political or cultural. What the film deals with is the impossibility to cultivate any identity (personal or collective).'[64] This is confirmed by the focus on exclusion as a major trope of *La Haine*, which stages scenes of literal exclusion that mirror the social and cultural exclusion of the characters. 'Motherfucker, we are locked in outside!' ('Nique sa mère, on est enfermés dehors!') exclaims Saïd after a taxi driver refuses to take them on with what he rightly suspects is a stolen credit card. Saïd's witticism could serve as a motto for the film, in which the heroes are constantly being thrown out of somewhere: out of the hospital, out of Astérix's flat, out of a nightclub and out of the art gallery. When they try to force their way into Astérix's block of flats, Kassovitz has the concierge pointedly say: 'Do you think the world belongs to you?' – anticipating the bitter irony of Saïd modifying the 'The World is Yours' poster to 'The World is Ours'. These are familiar images of

The television journalists

Vinz caught in their camera

The trio in the video entry-phone

News of Abdel's death broadcast

exclusion, found in many *banlieue* films, common enough to have become cliché. In *Douce France*, in a good example of stereotype appropriation, the *beur* hero says he curled his hair to look more *beur* so he would be thrown out of nightclubs, 'in order to integrate into exclusion'.

In the end, despite the sharp division between *banlieue* and city centre, the lack of social depth in the film means that the heroes are as excluded 'at home' as they are in the metropolis. In the first part of the film they have a dynamic and intimate relationship with the space around them, yet they spend time in liminal spaces such as playgrounds, rooftops and cellars. In sequence 4, a piece of graffiti behind their backs says 'No future'. They are under surveillance, constantly attempting to escape control. This is why the police order the youngsters off the rooftop in the *cité*, despite the fact that, as Nordine points out, they are doing nothing wrong. This surveillance, primarily by the police, is relayed symbolically in the film by CCTV cameras, by intercom, and is echoed and magnified by the ubiquitous eye of television.

Violence and the media gaze

Events in *La Haine*, especially violent events, are filtered, through film (the montage) and – more frequently – television. The emblematic figure of Abdel is distanced in this way: news of his coma is announced on television while his death is broadcast – immediately following images of Bosnia – on a giant screen in the empty shopping mall of Les Halles (sequence 16). The riots, too, are evoked through the film montage and then on television, rather than 'live'. There are prosaic reasons for not filming the riots themselves, which 'would have cost too much'.[65] However, this also enables the film to reflect on the place that violence occupies in contemporary media, especially when it comes to the *banlieue*, a reflection that shows both understanding of a social issue and an ambiguous relation to it.

When Hubert angrily tells the television journalists filming the *cité* that 'this is not Thoiry', he is alluding to a safari theme park near Paris, but also to the self-reinforcing media hunger for *banlieue* violence. In his analysis of space in *banlieue* films Adrian Fielder argues that the three heroes' hostility to the television journalists expresses 'both a consciousness of their confinement within the space delimited by the eye of the camera, and a desire to escape the scrutiny of this reifying gaze'.[66] This is true, yet the film also registers the fact that the representation of violence flatters their narcissism: Vinz is obsessed with watching the riots on television, and is annoyed that a friend of his was caught by the camera rather than himself. In other words, he is furious at the television journalists' attempt to portray him as a delinquent, yet in the next scene (at Darty's) he wishes he had been framed exactly as such. In Chapter 1 we saw how this dilemma informs the representation of *banlieue* 'problems' in real life. As the Marseille-based rap group IAM put it, 'The use of violence among the young is a concrete reality, not a myth. There are guns everywhere. And that's in part because of the stupid stereotypes carried by American films. [...] Yet violence constitutes the surest and most efficient way to be noticed, to come out of the crowd.'[67]

The same argument can be applied both to the characters in *La Haine* and to the film itself. It is no accident that Vinz, the most aggressive of the three leads, is the star of the film, and *La Haine*'s aura of macho aggression undoubtedly contributed to its worldwide success. By contrast, the more 'realistic' but more muted violence of the *beur* films did not export. Michael Medved has argued that dominant cinema favours violent material, even though the most successful films at the box office are 'family films'. As he points out, in 1994, for instance, *The Lion King* made three times more money than *Pulp Fiction*, yet it is the latter that attracted attention. For filmmakers and critics alike, 'respect is often granted to the most violent

References to *Scarface*: the 'The World is Yours' poster and Saïd altering it

Vinz in the mirror, imitating Robert De Niro in *Taxi Driver*

Reference to *Raging Bull*: 'Your mother sucks bears'

and disturbing fare'.[68] The worth of *La Haine* (like that of *Pulp Fiction*) cannot be reduced to its violence, but undoubtedly the latter helped both films' phenomenal success. Another reason for the success of *La Haine*, unlike other French *banlieue* films, was that it harnessed its 'local' message to international modes of representation.

A transnational film

An international film...

Following in the footsteps of Hitchcock and Godard, Kassovitz playfully inserts a cameo of himself in *La Haine* – as the skinhead beaten up by Vinz. As discussed in Chapter 1, there are other cameos, in particular his producer Christophe Rossignon and his father. For French film and television aficionados, there is also a range of in-jokes. The attempt to 'switch off' the Eiffel Tower (sequence 15) is a reference to a similar scene in Eric Rochant's *Un monde sans pitié*. Saïd's exchange with Vinz's sister at the beginning of the film, when she repeats 'pour quoi faire?' ('what for?') alludes to a sketch by French television comics 'Les Inconnus'. Most references, however, are quite explicitly American.

The protagonists' clothes, music and cinematic references are visibly and audibly American-influenced. Their language, too, includes American imports such as 'bâtard' ('bastard') and American references command respect, from *Lethal Weapon* to haircuts. As discussed in Chapter 3, these and other details – Darty wearing a T-shirt inscribed with 'Elvis shot JFK', the break-dancing scene – have struck American commentators as derivative, comic or passé. Particularly critical is Karen Alexander,[69] who sees the import of American culture as depoliticising and links the film to 'trendy fashion spreads', while Carrie Tarr[70] queries Kassovitz's legitimacy in using black American culture, on account of his white bourgeois background. Yet *La Haine*'s 'exploitation' of commodified forms of black American culture is 'political' precisely in showing the extent to which American culture has penetrated French youth culture. Despite struggles to assert French language and 'cultural exception' in the face of American 'invasion', French culture, especially working-class culture, is increasingly Americanised. Additionally, as we saw in Chapter 1, forms of black American culture – hip-hop in particular – have become strong markers of identity for *banlieue* youth. Thus, to a large extent the anxieties around the 'mimicry' of American culture by *La Haine* are expressions of nostalgia for some pure, archaic form of French culture. Additionally, a sense of what French cinema 'should be', steeped in the auteur films of the new wave, is reluctant to accept popular French culture for what it really is. Looking more closely at *La Haine*, we can detect a dual American import: the cinephilic slant of the director on the one hand and the working-class subculture of the characters on the other, but also strong differences between the film and the models it 'mimics'.

Kassovitz's first love was the American cinema of Spielberg, Scorsese, Lee, Tarantino and De Palma, and *La Haine* makes references to a number of their films. The introduction of the three main characters alludes to that of the heroes of *Mean Streets*, whose names are superimposed over their images at the beginning of the film – not surprising for a director who quotes *Mean Streets* as his 'favourite film'.[71] As befits the postmodern era, Kassovitz's homage is filtered through another: 'I found it annoying in *Reservoir Dogs* that [Tarantino] should copy Scorsese. So I tried to do something different, it's a little joke.'[72] Certainly, Vinz and Saïd's aggressive command of space and verbal delivery recalls Scorsese's heroes. As Susan Morrison has noted, there are parallels: 'Fluid camera; [...] a reliance on idiosyncratic male actors like De Niro and Keitel; a carefully selected and coded soundtrack and a near-hysterical tension lying just beneath the surface, ready to erupt at any moment.'[73] Anecdotally, one can also quote details such as the insult tagged on the wall of Hubert's gym ('Your mother sucks bears'), which recalls Joe Pesci's outburst on the telephone in *Raging Bull* ('Your mother sucks big elephant dicks'), and Vinz's Jewishness can be compared to the Italian-Americans of both Scorsese's and Lee's films. More generally, violent American genres are referenced, for instance the discussion of the stolen gun in relation to the *Lethal Weapon* series, and the various references to *Scarface*: Astérix's cocaine snorting refers to the 1983 De Palma version, the 'The World is Yours' poster to Howard Hawks' 1932 film.

There are, however, important differences between the way Kassovitz films his situation, characters and – especially – violence and his American 'models' that make his film not an imitation but, like Jean-Pierre Melville's French thrillers of the 1960s, a reworking that bears marks of French tradition. Interestingly, one of the most important differences is the playing down of violence. As Olivier Seguret has put it: 'Where an American film would not have hesitated to spectacularise violence, Kassovitz on the contrary develops a *mise en scène* which while being admittedly "speeded-up", is in the end very sober.'[74] Indeed, as discussed earlier, actual violence is alluded to and filtered through self-reflexive representation, rather than directly – except in the police station scene, though this is minimal and mediated by the young policeman's gaze. While this could be attributed to the smaller budget, other instances point to a deliberate stylistic choice. For instance, the beating up of the skinhead is shot in medium to long shot in a dark courtyard at night, the close-up of Kassovitz's bloody face no more than a few seconds. It is also instructive to compare the 'Mexican stand-off' at the end of *La Haine* with the same motif in John Woo's films. In *The Killer* (1989) the Mexican stand-off is repeatedly, lovingly, showcased. The situation of two men holding each other at gunpoint becomes an extended and spectacular *mise en scène* leitmotif that is declined in different registers: surprise, suspense, terror, and – in the scene between the killer and his friend/nemesis policeman with the blind heroine – it even includes a comic element. By contrast, for its only occurrence at the end of *La Haine* it is held for a mere 35 seconds, between two static characters, with no music, before the screen goes black. As we observed earlier in the discussion of the narrative fate of the characters, this indicates that the film's interest lies more with a collective, social and symbolic violence than with individual, bloody infighting.

There is also an interesting slippage in several cinematic references that the film indulges in: Kassovitz makes his heroes inhabit his own cinematic and visual culture rather than theirs. Vinz talking to himself in his bathroom mirror imitates the 1977 hero of *Taxi Driver*, where a similar young man in 1995 would more likely have copied Bruce Willis or Arnold Schwarzenegger (similarly, the heroes' discussion of *Pif* and *Hercule*, French Communist comics characters dating back to the 1950s, strikes as relating to Kassovitz's rather than the three heroes' culture). Kassovitz acknowledges this discrepancy when discussing his use of 'The World is Yours' from *Scarface*: 'I put that in because everyone on those estates knows De Palma's *Scarface*. As soon as you mention the movies, they say, "Oh yeah, just like in *Scarface*." Naturally, they don't know the original.'[75] (In fact, in De Palma's film 'The World is Yours' is no longer a poster but a garish brass and pink neon statue, which stands over the pool in which the hero collapses after he is shot.) Similarly, the references to Spike Lee are also evidence of Kassovitz's cinephilia rather than *banlieue* tastes.

It is through such a skilful blend of American and French influences that *La Haine* achieved its international impact. While retaining a clear connection to a French social situation and characters, in narrative, stylistic and ideological terms Kassovitz also harnessed this national slant to an international idiom. His subsequent career, which took him to Hollywood, would show to what extent he later successfully mastered the codes of violent American genre cinema (see Chapter 3).

... But also a French film

Having discussed the transnational aspect of the film, it is time to bring it back for the last time to its French context. Set among the inhabitants of a deprived *banlieue* on the outskirts of Paris, *La Haine* offers a particularly noir vision of its 'proletarian' heroes. In 1930s Poetic Realist films and in 1970s social comedies and dramas, the protagonists – typically played by such actors as the young Jean Gabin in *Le Jour se lève* (1939) and the young Gérard Depardieu in *Les Valseuses* (1974) – related to a proletarian community and were alienated from its establishment, pitted against middle-aged, bourgeois figures in front of whom they represented youthful (and rightful) rebellion. In *La Haine*, 20 years on from *Les Valseuses*, there is no longer a community to relate to or be alienated from.

Beyond hip-hop and sports clothes, beyond admiration for Hollywood, looms another kind of American influence, that of the neo-capitalism and abdication of state social responsibility that created the American ghettos. Though state welfare is still substantial in France (and was at the time the film was made), the most pessimistic predictions saw the 'inverse utopia'[76] of the American ghettos as the future world order: a growing underclass of *exclus* (excluded people) who, as summed up by François Dubet, 'live in several worlds at the same time [...] in economic exclusion and in a society of consumption'.[77] The characters in *La Haine* are such *exclus*, caught in this vicious contradiction between disavowal of capitalism and avowal of consumerism, symbolised, for instance, by Santo, Vinz and friends cruising in a BMW but excluded from a nightclub. The beginning of *La Haine* is about 1990s demonstrations that themselves recalled 1960s political struggles. Yet the film's heroes are politically disengaged and have no social conscience: for example, they show zero compassion for a woman beggar in the Métro. Unlike the characters in the Marxist *État des lieux* with a well-articulated political programme, but like many others in the films of the *jeune cinéma français*, they are anomic, helpless and hopeless; this is visualised in the way they sit in an amorphous way, especially in the first half of the film. Their aggression, against the police and other institutions, is visceral, random and self-defeating, as the ending so shockingly shows. We are no longer in the Communist 'red suburbs' of the 1960s; in this respect, *État des lieux* is sadly anachronistic. The neo-capitalist 'malaise des *banlieues*' of the 1990s is rather a throwback to the 19th-century 'dangerous classes', the hordes of 'savage' *apaches* menacing bourgeois society from the fringes of the city. The film's chilling ending takes place under giant murals representing the *maudit* romantic figures of Baudelaire and Rimbaud, put in place by the well-meaning architects of Chanteloup-les-Vignes. Kassovitz alleges that he 'did not know who [the murals] represented'.[78] Even if this were true (which I doubt), this symbolic visual placement cruelly underlines the failure of the cultural policies that were supposed to help the *cités*, and his heroes' alienation from the figure of the romantic rebel as well as from any historical change.

The question is: does *La Haine* provide a clear-sighted portrayal of this situation, or is it caught in its contradictions? Does it criticise or celebrate its heroes' ideological alienation and confusion? Does its stylistic sophistication, its spectacular pleasures, undercut its 'authenticity'? The answer, of course, in each case is that it does both. For Vincent Amiel, the *jeune cinéma français* in general tends to 'cut itself off from social representations, through an excess of style'.[79] Many others (as detailed in Chapter 3) have, on the contrary, seen *La Haine* as the indictment of an explosive social situation. If, as I have argued, the contents of the film did not really offer new insight, its style and stylishness do. *La Haine* has an equal urge to enlighten and to entertain, and it does so in a fresh and internationally understandable way. Its stylistic pleasures do not undercut its authenticity but, on the contrary, enable it to travel. Its ideological contradictions – between youth who are excluded and angry and yet enslaved by consumerism, between the lure of media spectacularisation and its traps – are themselves typical of an age where the grand narratives of politics and history have disappeared. We are a long way from the committed cinema Kassovitz's own father was involved in, in the 1960s. There has been a 'return to the political', and certainly to 'the social', in French cinema of the 1990s, but *La Haine* is not at its forefront. With the benefit of hindsight, we also know that this is not at all the direction Kassovitz himself followed (as discussed at the end of Chapter 3). Nevertheless, the energy, youthful zest and brilliance of its style, the charisma of its performers, but also ultimately its sincerity have made *La Haine* an important and unforgettable film.

Notes

1   'Interview with Mathieu Kassovitz' in Ciment and Herpe (eds), *Projections 9*, p. 190.
2   Ibid., p. 191.
3   *L'Express*, 11 May 1995.
4   'Interview with Mathieu Kassovitz', p. 184.
5   Beugnet, Martine, *Marginalité, sexualité, contrôle dans le cinéma français contemporain*. Paris, L'Harmattan, 2000, p. 14.
6   CRS stands for 'Compagnies Républicaines de Sécurité'. The CRS were created at the Liberation to restore order and used to repress strikes and other unrest, for instance during the Algerian war. They acquired a notorious reputation with the repression of the May 1968 student events.
7   Ciment and Herpe, 'Interview with Mathieu Kassovitz', p. 189.
8   Konstantarakos, Myrto, 'Which mapping of the city? *La Haine* (Kassovitz, 1995) and the *cinéma de banlieue*', in P. Powrie (ed.), *French Cinema in the 1990s*, p. 162.
9   Ciment and Herpe, 'Interview with Mathieu Kassovitz', p. 185.

10 At the time of *La Haine*, this could have been a reference to *Lethal Weapon 1* (1987), *Lethal Weapon 2* (1989) and *Lethal Weapon 3* (1992) – all directed by Richard Donner.

11 Ciment and Herpe, 'Interview with Mathieu Kassovitz', p. 184.

12 Ebert, Roger, *The Chicago Sun-Times*, 4 April 1996.

13 *Mise en abyme* (or *mise en abîme*), initially a term of rhetoric, means the embedding of one story into another, or of one process into another.

14 Kassovitz, Mathieu, commentary, Canal+ DVD, *La Haine*, 2001.

15 Information for this section comes from Kassovitz's commentary, Canal+ DVD, 2001.

16 Taubin, Amy, 'Primal screen', *The Village Voice*, 2–8 August 2000.

17 Perkins, V.F., *Film as Film: Understanding and Judging Movies*. Harmondsworth, Penguin, 1972, p. 45.

18 Kelly, Richard, *The Name of this Book is Dogme95*. London, Faber & Faber, 2000, p. 9.

19 Dyer, Richard, *White*. London and New York, Routledge, 1997, pp. 98–99.

20 A notable exception is Jean-François Richet's film *État des lieux*.

21 These scenes are visible as supplements on the Canal+ DVD *La Haine*, 2001.

22 Boulay, Anne and Colmant, Marie, *Libération*, 31 May 1995.

23 Aumont, Jacques and Marie, Michel, *Dictionnaire théorique et critique du cinéma*. Paris, Nathan, 2001, p. 158.

24 Bordwell, David, 'Intensified continuity: visual style in contemporary American film', *Film Quarterly*, Spring 2002.

25 Ciment and Herpe, 'Interview with Mathieu Kassovitz', p. 188

26 Ibid., p. 191

27 Canal+ DVD, *La Haine*, 2001.

28 Rémy, interview with Mathieu Kassovitz.

29 J.D., 'interview du fanzine *Steadycam*'.

30 In the commentary on the Canal+ DVD, Kassovitz indicates that he went as far as a painting a plastic bag in reverse to suggest its mirror image.

31 J.D., 'interview du fanzine *Steadycam*'.

32 Canal+ DVD.

33 Ciment and Herpe, 'Interview with Mathieu Kassovitz', p. 189.

34 Ibid., p. 188.

35 Ibid., p. 192.

36 Mongin, Olivier, 'Regarde les tomber; à propos de *La Haine*', *Esprit*, August–September 1995, p. 178.

37 Ciment and Herpe, 'Interview with Mathieu Kassovitz', p. 192

38 Tranchant, Marie-Noelle, *Le Figaro*, 27 May 1995.

39 A brief extract from Edith Piaf's 'Je ne regrette rien', 'sampled' by the DJ. Piaf's song could be doubly ironic, as a symbol of populist Frenchness, and as the anthem of ultra-right paratroopers during the Algerian war.

40 Rémy, interview with Mathieu Kassovitz.

41 'Interview with Mathieu Kassovitz', p. 190. Kassovitz elsewhere argues that '[S]omeone who is angry, who has "hatred" because he lives in an estate, has nothing to do with a skinhead who believes in a totalitarian ideology'. But the similarity remains; in Ferenczi, Aurelien, *InfoMatin*, 31 May 1995.

42 Seguret, Olivier, *Libération*, 29 May 1995.

43 Konstantarakos, 'Which mapping of the city?', p. 166.

44   The tracksuit is gold-coloured, as visible in the cut scenes on the Canal+ DVD.
45   Begag, 'L'enfermement linguistique', p. 7.
46   Rémy, interview with Mathieu Kassovitz.
47   For a further analysis of this scene, see Higbee, Will, 'Screening the "other" Paris: cinematic representations of the French urban periphery in *La Haine* and *Ma 6-T Va Crack-er*', *Modern and Contemporary France*, 9, (2), 2001, pp. 197–208.
48   Ferenczi, *InfoMatin*, 31 May 1995.
49   Rosello, Mireille, *Declining the Stereotype*. Hanover, NH and London, University Press of New England, 1998, p. 66.
50   Tarr, Carrie, 'Ethnicity and identity in *Métisse* and *La Haine* by Mathieu Kassovitz', in T. Chafer (ed.), *Multicultural France*, Working Paper on Contemporary France no. 7, University of Portsmouth, 1997, pp. 40–47.
51   His fantasies, as well as his Jewishness, are extra-textually associated with the director, who has in various interviews referred to the cow hallucination as a tribute to his anarchist grandfather: 'Mort aux vaches' – 'Death to the cows' – is an old anarchist motto, 'cows' signifying the police.
52   Rosello, *Declining the Stereotype*, p. 8.
53   Levieux, Michèle, *L'Humanité*, 29 May 1995.
54   Stafford, Roy, *La Haine* (*Hate*), York Film Notes. London, York Press, 2000, p. 23.
55   For Mongin, Astérix signifies the world of male prostitution, in which Saïd would be implicated. This seems to me unlikely. Apart from a reference by Astérix to Saïd as to whether his brother 'still fucks', there is no clear evidence that Saïd is involved in male prostitution, especially in view of his lack of sexual experience, which is mocked by his friends. Mongin, 'Regarde-les tomber', p. 177.
56   *L'Express*, 11 May 1995.
57   Ibid.
58   *Première*, June 1995, p. 111.
59   The narrowly sexual characterisation of women is illustrated further on the CD 'inspired' by the film, where the only female performer sings of prostitution.
60   Mahoney, Elisabeth, '"The People in Parentheses": Space under pressure in the post-modern city', in D.B. Clarke (ed.), *The Cinematic City*. London, Routledge, 1997, p. 178.
61   J.D., 'interview du fanzine *Steadycam*'.
62   Darty is the name of an electronic goods store.
63   J.D., 'interview du fanzine *Steadycam*'.
64   Mongin, 'Regarde-les tomber', *Esprit*, p. 173. A note on translation: Mongin uses the words 'Républicain', which I have rendered as 'political', and 'culturaliste', which I have rendered as 'cultural'. Although the words have more specific meaning in the French context, I have opted for clarity.
65   'Interview with Mathieu Kassovitz', p. 192.
66   Fielder, Adrian, 'Poaching on public space: urban autonomous zones in the French banlieue films', in M. Shiel and T. Fitzmaurice (eds), *Cinema and the City: Film and Urban Societies in a Global Context*. Oxford and Malden, MA Blackwell, 2001, p. 274.
67   *Les Inrockuptibles*, 31 May 1995.
68   Medved, Michael, 'Hollywood's four big lies', in K. French (ed.), *Screen Violence*. London, Bloomsbury, 1996, p. 29.

69 Alexander, Karen, '*La Haine*', *Vertigo*, Autumn/Winter 1995, pp. 42–47.

70 Carrie Tarr, 'Ethnicity and identity in *Métisse* and *La Haine*'. See also a later piece: Tarr, Carrie, 'Ethnicity and identity in the *cinéma de banlieue*', in P. Powrie, *Cinema on the Urban Margin*, Powrie (ed.), *French Cinema in the 1990s*, pp. 172–184.

71 Ciment and Herpe, 'Interview with Mathieu Kassovitz', p. 185.

72 Ibid., p. 190.

73 Morrison, Susan, '*La Haine, Fallen Angels*, and some thoughts on Scorsese's children', *CineAction!*, December 1995, p. 46.

74 *Libération*, 29 May 1995.

75 'Interview with Mathieu Kassovitz', p. 190.

76 Wacquant, 'De L'Amérique comme utopie à l'envers'.

77 Dubet, François, quoted in Boucher, Manuel, 'Rap and the combination logics of rogues', in A.P. Durand (ed.), *Black, Blanc, Beur*, p. 69.

78 *L'Express*, 11 May 95.

79 Amiel, 'Une nouvelle génération', p. 104.

3 Box office and critical reception

I've been living on that movie for the past ten years. I've done so many things in between, but nobody cares. It's my curse. It's also something I'm very proud of.

Mathieu Kassovitz, presentation for the re-release of *La Haine*, The Screen on the Green cinema, London, 17 August 2004

Reception in France

Box office and audience reactions

In early February 1995 Mathieu Kassovitz showed *La Haine* to his crew and cast, and in late March the first press screenings registered enthusiastic reactions. Gilles Jacob, director of the Cannes festival, wanted the film for the *Un certain regard* section (where new, or unusual auteur films traditionally belong), but Lazennec pressed for it to be part of the official selection. This was agreed only a few days before the beginning of the festival. *La Haine* was on its way.

Even before the Cannes showing, Kassovitz was in the news; press coverage took off as the Cannes selection was announced: 'For ten days, Mathieu Kassovitz does interview upon interview: *Positif, Première, Télérama, Le Point, L'Express, Les Inrockuptibles, Le Journal du Dimanche*, etc. Demand is exceptional and pressure rises around the film'.[1] Kassovitz also appeared on television, including the popular live literary show 'Bouillon de culture' on 26 May, the day before the official Cannes screening. On it, Kassovitz wore a cap with a cannabis leaf design and refused to take it off when a viewer rang on behalf of an anti-drugs organisation. The mini-scandal followed him to Cannes, where the triumphant screening of the film created media madness; for *Studio Magazine*, it was 'almost like the Beatles'.[2] The film itself had, in journalistic terms, 'the effect of a 'bomb'.[3] While *La Haine* received a 'standing ovation at its morning screening'.[4] *Libération* reported that '[A]fter the evening gala screening […] uniformed police supposed to form a double ceremonial parade outside were unable to hide their contempt: they ostentatiously looked towards the sea, in other words they turned a hateful back to the team who made the film that hates them'.[5] Meanwhile, Kassovitz and his crew played up their 'young' image to the hilt, throwing a cocktail party with Coca-Cola, beer and merguez sausages rather than the customary champagne and canapés. At the awards ceremony the film won the Best Director prize (having also been nominated for the Golden Palm), thus moving up one more ratchet in the celebrity stakes.

Three days later, on 31 May, *La Haine* was released, attracting an exceptional 21,000 spectators in Paris alone. Most daily papers featured the film and director on the front page.[6] Quickly, cashing in on the buzz from Cannes, 260 prints were distributed nationally instead of the planned 50, the publicity campaign featuring a striking, punchy set of posters. For a film about the police and violence, Kassovitz had wanted a poster that was 'hard, without advertising logos. […] One must retain integrity'.[7] One unused design shows Vinz's fist aggressively thrust in close-up[8] and the three young men in the background. Kassovitz also rejected the image of a gun, replacing it with the angry eyes of the three heroes,[9] in a set of three black and white posters, each featuring the harsh gaze of one of the main protagonists at the top, a black band in the middle with the title in white and, at the bottom, a band of three images of riots and police. The accusing gaze of the young men advertised the 'hard' stance of the film, pointing the finger at 'society', while the images at the bottom, evoking the opening montage, reinforced the anti-police message and a semi-documentary look. The refusal of logos notwithstanding, the posters featured the Cannes prize and, in later versions (reproduced, for instance, on the VHS and DVD), the Best Film and/or Best Editing César prizes were also indicated. Although each of the three young men featured on one of the posters, it is interesting that the ones most frequently reproduced (in the press, on the VHS or DVD) are those featuring, first, Vincent Cassel and, second, Hubert Koundé, echoing the hierarchy of the characters in the film itself, as discussed in Chapter 2. Apart from an effective poster, the film benefited from an unusual degree of merchandising for a French film, making Kassovitz's later complaints of media 'recuperation' slightly disingenuous. The script was published as an illustrated book, and two CDs were released: one including the soundtrack of both *La Haine* and *Métisse*, and a CD of rap music 'inspired' by *La Haine* and featuring popular French rap artists such as Ministère Amer, IAM and Assassin (and MC Solaar on some versions).[10] A photographic exhibition was mounted at La Villette in Paris. Later, *La Haine* gift T-shirts were produced to accompany the sale of the VHS.

The film went over the 2,000,000 spectator mark at the domestic box office, an excellent score in an already successful year for French cinema. Although the statistics compiled by *Studio Magazine* place *La Haine* at no. 5 at the national box office for 1995, more complete and definitive statistics (which include films released in November and December and thus not part of the *Studio* statistics) show *La Haine* at no. 14, thus still in the top 20 for 1995. It was, unsurprisingly, beaten by French comedies with popular stars (the top five films of that somewhat miraculous year include no fewer than four French comedies, among them *Les Anges gardiens*, with Gérard Depardieu, and *Gazon Maudit*, by and with Josiane Balasko), and international blockbusters (*Die Hard 3*, *Goldeneye*, *Pocahontas*, *Apollo 13*). But *La Haine* was also ahead of other Hollywood films, such as *Batman Forever* and of popular auteur films, for instance *Nelly and M. Arnaud* and *Il postino*, which both featured major stars. Given its absence of stars, famous director, large budget or special effects, *La Haine* was thus the true surprise hit of its year.[11]

While *La Haine* did exceptionally well at the box office, its release was in other ways eventful. Some screenings provoked violent reactions from sections of the audience close to the milieu depicted in the film – turning rough in places such as Sarcelles, a large working-class suburb north of Paris, but also at cinemas in central Paris and Marseille. Even at the Grand Rex in Paris (a huge, prestige first-run cinema) gangs of youths succeeded in cheating their way in and disrupting screenings by smoking and loud comments. *Télérama* quotes some young people as saying: 'We want to say that we exist, not burn cars. For once the cinema gives us this opportunity.'[12] In Marseille, similar problems occurred, for instance at the UGC cinema in

CRS riot police in opening montage

'Police kill' graffiti in opening montage

The police station after the riot

Saïd and Hubert brutally manhandled while a third policeman watches

the centre of the city, where seats were broken.[13] In Marseille, too, Kassovitz and the owner of the art cinema the César (which once belonged to Marcel Pagnol) were 'copiously insulted' and Vincent Cassel booed off stage for being a 'slave to the star system'.[14] The film and the team also got mixed reactions when Kassovitz organised special screenings for youths from La Noë and other similar *cités*. Although the screenings for the inhabitants of La Noë garnered warm applause and requests for autographs, the crew encountered some hostility from other *cité* dwellers. A young spectator from Saint-Denis (another northern working-class suburb) said: 'I saw a lot of caricatures in your film. [...] But it is especially the media hype around the film that gets on my nerves. Where do those journalists live, to be able to tell whether *La Haine* is realistic?'[15] Another commented, 'Your film is ten years out of date. Kids on the estates are no longer dazzled by guns. You get young kids aged 9 or 10 dealing in drugs, so...La *banlieue* is not a fiction! The line in the film where Vinz says "I am not Malik Oussekine" [the young *beur* 'accidentally' killed by a policeman in 1986] stinks. Do you think Oussekine had any choice?' And then, somewhat self-contradictorily, 'Events in films like yours I can see every day on my estate.'[16] Elsewhere, young people also criticised the characters: 'We are not idiots, unlike the young people in the film'; 'Look at the cretin making faces in front of his mirror, do I do this when I get up in the morning?'; 'They made us look like fools and monkeys.' And another: 'When I walk in the street, I know what people think if they have seen *La Haine*. [...] This film should be burnt.'[17]

More positive reactions are recorded in a *Télérama* survey about *banlieue* youths who had come to see the film at regular showings at the Pathé Wepler, a large cinema on Place Clichy in central Paris. On Whitsun Monday, the audience was composed of 'a mixture of Vinz, Hubert and Saïd lookalikes', spectators who rarely went to the cinema in Paris, or indeed at all; the manager commented, 'The audience is not the one we normally see: they are young people who come in gangs, not necessarily from the same area. But the screenings have a cohesive effect... There is a real identification effect.' One youthful spectator said that, compared to his local cinema in Aulnay-sous-bois, north-east of Paris, 'Here you can buy Coca-Cola and popcorn, as in America. In any case I never go to the cinema. But this is different, it talks about us.' Another indicates approval of the film but hatred of media attitudes, in a less virulent version of some of the reactions noted above and of those of three heroes of the film: 'La Haine is real life. This is how it is where we live. But we don't have to talk to journalists. We are not animals in a zoo.' And, for some, 'Kassovitz's dialogue is exaggerated. We do not speak like this, with an obscenity per sentence. On the other hand the attitude of the cops is well portrayed.'[18] The same report also points out that, in the month following the release of the film, 'Teachers joined the fray: in Saint-Denis, since the beginning of June, whole classrooms have come to see the film. This is probably a way of calming everyone after the events of Noisy-le-Grand.'

This last remark refers to violent riots on 8 and 9 June 1995 in the Butte-Verte cité in Noisy-le-Grand, east of Paris, provoked by the death of a young Beur, Belkacem Belhabib, who crashed his motorbike while being chased by the police – a set of events that somehow parallels those of the film. Coming so soon after the release of La Haine, the Noisy-le-Grand riots were inevitably seen as 'copycat', involving the film in a debate about its 'responsibility' and that of the media in general in the violence engulfing society: France-Soir of 9 June neatly entitled its story 'Noisy-la-haine', and the Front National leader Jean-Marie Le Pen exclaimed: 'Do these yobs have la haine? Send them to jail!'[19] François Dubet, an academic and sociologist renowned for his work on the banlieues,[20] was asked to study the phenomenon, but wisely concluded: 'One must not overestimate the role of cinema or television. The banlieue kids did not wait for La Haine to express themselves. After Les Minguettes, Vaulx-en-Velin, Lille or Rouen, it is yet again the same scenario that was reproduced in Noisy-le-Grand. [...] I do not wish to stigmatise journalists, but the logic of information is that of the spectacular.'[21]

While all this was taking place President Chirac had sent an appreciative letter to Kassovitz, and Prime Minister Alain Juppé asked for the film to be screened to government officials. Together with the overwhelming publicity, the fact that Kassovitz was required to be in some way accountable beyond the effect of a 'normal' film seems to have gone to his head. His insolent replies to interviewers at Cannes and afterwards, combined with inexperience and youthful awkwardness, provoked something of a backlash – the most visible expression of which was his satirisation as one of the puppets in the popular 'Guignols' show on Canal+, which, as Studio Magazine says, best summed up his predicament 'by caricaturing him permanently hesitating between his desire to shout his opinions loud and clear and his desire to remain discreet'.[22] But if *La Haine* was, as we can see, a true *phénomène de société*, it was also appreciated as a film. Its popular success matched its critical reception.

A rare critical consensus

From the moment it was selected for the Cannes festival, *La Haine* generated an abundant press and an extraordinarily positive critical consensus. This consensus, unusual in the French context spanned the spectrum of the French press in two directions, from the trade and popular press to the cinephile journals on the one hand, and across political opinions on the other. For instance, the right-wing *Le Figaro magazine* of 10 June 1996, even as it used the film as a pretext to berate the dangers of immigration and government failure, conceded that it was 'well made and well acted' and that it 'did not exaggerate' the issues [namely violence in the suburbs, etc.] it shows'.[23]

This critical consensus focused on three main areas: the discovery of a new auteur in Kassovitz, the 'correct' and novel representation of the social issues the film deals with, and *La Haine*'s cinematic qualities. Across the press Kassovitz was hailed as that most precious commodity in French cinema, a new auteur, a figurehead in the 'new wave' of *jeune cinéma français* (see Chapter 1), with a distinctive style, his energetic editing and use of black and white being particularly noted. The reference to the new wave of the late 1950s and early 1960s is clear in, among others, Alain Riou's review in *Le Nouvel Observateur*: 'Like *À bout de souffle* in its time, *La Haine* marks the emergence of a different cinema, the cinema we were waiting for.'[24] This view is endorsed by many, including the actor Jean-Pierre Cassel (Vincent's father), who says that 'people like Vincent and Mathieu Kassovitz, are a real new wave'.[25] In general, for critics across the board, the film 'traces an avenue for the future of French cinema'.[26] The young director's talent is praised to high heaven; he is, in the words of *France-Soir*'s reviewer, the 'super-gifted child of French cinema'.[27] As several reviewers also point out, Kassovitz with *La Haine* is a shining exception to the rule whereby brilliant and original first films are followed by disappointing second movies: 'Contrary to the general curse, *La Haine* is far superior to *Métisse*, Kassovitz' first feature film, which it surpasses at the same time as it erases its faults.'[28] As we saw, *La Haine* was made on a much higher budget than *Métisse*, and it is undoubtedly a more sophisticated and accomplished film; however, perhaps unwittingly, one reviewer points to another reason why *La Haine* would be celebrated above *Métisse*: 'The disappointing, cloyingly right-on trio [of central characters] in *Métisse* is swept away by the explosive threesome of *La Haine*.'[29] In other words, *La Haine*'s more complex – but also more ambivalent – approach to race paid off in a country where upfront ideological approaches are frequently confused with (negatively viewed) 'political correctness'. We may also speculate that the fact that the 'explosive' trio was all male was preferred to the more feminine *Métisse*, which with the hindsight of a further decade turns out to be something of an exception in Kassovitz's work.

In this context, *La Haine*, more surprisingly, also achieved consensus in relation to its social contents. Reference is frequently made, approvingly, to the fact that the film was inspired by the real case of Makome M'Bowole as well as more distant *bavures* such as the death of Malik Oussekine in 1986, and to the film's indictment of police brutality. Together with the extensive use of *verlan*, all this is noted with approval. But, above all, Kassovitz is praised for adopting an 'uncompromising' and 'truthful' approach to the socially deprived youth of the Parisian *banlieue*, and, more widely, the *fracture sociale* endemic in the mid-1990s. For *L'Express*, Kassovitz 'turns his uncompromising camera on to a black and white chronicle of a predictable social explosion... [H]e is brave.'[30] For *Le Nouvel Observateur*, Kassovitz 'understood that the number one topic in France, the only one worth treating, is this famous *fracture sociale* [and] he was curious enough to have a go at it'.[31] For *Les Echos*, the film 'rings terribly true'.[32] For *InfoMatin*, '[I]t is a long time since French cinema, stuck in its cosy conformity (characters living in opulent flats, obsessed with their love life), had shown our dysfunctional, sick society with such accuracy... *La Haine* is distinct from most representations of the *banlieue* and *cités*, which are either too well documented or too folkloric, haunted by *cinéma-vérité* or by an artificial miserabilism.'[33] I could go on and add other quotes (even the Communist daily *L'Humanité*, which warns in veiled terms of the dangers of demagogy in such a topic, ends up praising the film). The originality of *La Haine* was also seen to present its picture of the *fracture sociale* in a radically different way from the naturalistic or documentary style adopted by most filmmakers of 'social' subjects. Kassovitz's wedding of a new style to the topic in this respect is clearly behind much of this critical praise. For instance, *Télérama* recognises the originality of the film in these terms: 'A very successful attempt not to illustrate truth but to recreate it.'[34] As *InfoMatin* continues, *La Haine* 'is the kind of film in which, for the first time, form and content work hand in hand rather than fighting each other'.[35] In fact, such is the high currency of the film's style that the reviewer in *Les Inrockuptibles*, a trendy music-oriented journal normally harsh on any 'earnest' social representation, praises it for *not* being 'too realistic' and in ways that, yet again, restate the film's departure from 'usual' representations: 'The main quality of *La Haine* is precisely its wish to do away with the heavy panoply of the *film à thème*… [T]his is no sociological parade, we do not find the usual clichés about anti-youth neighbours, stupid vigilantes, or racial integration.'[36] As we saw in Chapter 1, numerous other French films had tackled the same topic, and, moreover, there are many similarities between events in *La Haine* and dominant television representations (the 'usual clichés'). This does make the claims for originality either excessive or ignorant, or an example of collective disavowal: stylistic originality meant that critics were blind to the contents.

As part of the praise for the film's style and stylishness, the performances of the central trio were lauded across the board as particularly impressive: 'The three lead actors… are wonderful';[37] the film 'is carried by vibrant actors' 'a dazzling trio of actors';[38] and so on. *Libération* singles out the scene in which Vinz imitates Robert De Niro in *Taxi Driver* in front of his bathroom mirror ('Are you talking to me'?) for special praise: 'In this quotation Cassel does not pale in front of his model De Niro, any more than Kassovitz in front of his, Scorsese.'[39] A scene that had been picked up by a young viewer as making the character appear as a 'cretin', as we saw above, was picked up by reviewers as a cinephile quotation.

The critical opinions discussed so far emanate on the whole from reviews and interviews in the non-specialist press, mostly daily and weekly mainstream newspapers. The remarkable thing about *La Haine* is that it also disarmed the usually much more cautious and demanding specialist film journals, which are frequently hostile to popular French cinema. Indeed, Kassovitz had been annoyed by *Cahiers du cinéma*'s dismissal of *Métisse*, as an 'ugly film, without ambition', and subsequently by the journal's use of *La Haine* on the cover of its June 1995 issue without his agreement. He even claims to have 'barred the *Cahiers* crowd from the first press screening of *La Haine*'.[40] Nevertheless, both *Cahiers du cinéma*[41] and *Positif*[42] enthusiastically championed the film and allotted it extra space beyond the normal review. *Cahiers* published a piece on the '*banlieue-films*' as well as a long and complimentary review by Thierry Jousse, which, while pointing to some political ambiguities in the film, praised it for its 'opening of a stylised window on French reality' and its avoidance of the 'trap of political correctness'.[43] *Cahiers* subsequently published a further piece on the film.[44] *Positif*, for its part, ran a long interview with Kassovitz, which was later published in English, and in a later issue ran a long piece on the film and the *banlieue* genre.[45] One should also mention here an extended commentary on the film by Olivier Mongin in the left-wing intellectual journal *Esprit*.[46] In opposition to the overall consensus, Mongin argued against seeing it as an anti-police film or a *film de banlieue*, though without offering a clear alternative reading (the piece is further discussed in Chapter 2). In this coverage we find the same themes as in the rest of the press: Kassovitz's growing auteur status, the film's 'praiseworthy' approach to its social topic, and its cinematic qualities. But, typical of the hostility of these auteurist journals to naturalism and classic 'social' cinema, like *Les Inrockuptibles* they praise *La Haine* for its ability, as *Cahiers* puts it, to 'escape naturalism' and 'avoid many pitfalls, notably that of demagogy on the *banlieue malaise* and *political correctness*' [italics in the original];[47] similarly, for *Positif*, '*La Haine* could have been only a committed film, and we should be thankful that it avoided simplistic and demagogic excess'.[48] These recurrent remarks give us another clue as to the reason for the consensus around *La Haine*: the film was sufficiently social in contents to appear hard-edged, but not too much, so that – in *Cahiers*' terms – it could 'escape naturalism'.

Meanwhile, the more popular French specialist film magazines such as *Studio Magazine* and *Première* – as was to be expected – lavished praise on the film. In line with their populist leaning and younger readers, they devoted more space to the actors and to anecdotes about the shooting as well as the team's youth. Even before *La Haine* was made, Kassovitz's age and rebellious reputation were rather complacently reiterated.[49] In early 1995 the shooting of the film in La Noë, the fact that the team had lived on the spot for two months and the problems they encountered were covered (after the event, as a result of Kassovitz's agreement with the mayor not to publicise the shoot at the time; in this respect we may note the absence of Chanteloup-les-Vignes on the end credits). As mentioned already, a massive number of interviews and articles were published in *Première* and *Studio Magazine* during Cannes, and then when the film came out. Further pieces followed – for instance, interviews with Kassovitz and the actors. In November 1995, *Première* asked Kassovitz to interview Emir Kusturica ('K par K'), who had taken the Palme d'Or that year at Cannes. In December 1995 the special end-of-year issue of *Studio Magazine* generously featured *La Haine* as one of the key films of the year; included was an entertaining 'diary' of *La Haine* before, during and after the Cannes festival. All this coverage celebrated the 'bold', 'burning' and 'courageous' nature of the project, without a breath of criticism. *Studio Magazine* concluded its review by saying: 'Rush and adore this film.'[50] The trade papers obviously also supported the film as one of the successes of 1995. In an extensive dossier on the state of French cinema, *Le Film Français* praised *La Haine* as one of the few French films 'cited by many exhibitors as the model of a French film that integrated American codes without losing its soul'.[51]

This critical consensus, which, it cannot be overemphasised, is very rare in France, was reflected in the awards showered on the film, which after the Best Direction prize at Cannes was given three Césars, having also been nominated in a record eight other categories (see Appendix 4). Paradoxically, the abundance of honours and the effusive press coverage became a problem for the director, who felt that his film was too universally saluted. As *Le Figaro* noted, 'Kassovitz ... would like his film to trigger off fights, provoke quarrels and polemics, but he only succeeds in generating a flattering buzz'. [...] '*La Haine*, which people love too much, is an embarrassment [to him].'[52] At the same time, some muted criticism of the film also surfaced, which, together with Kassovitz's unease, showed a few cracks in the veneer of universal acclaim.

Cracks in the consensus

A few reviewers[53] pointed to a couple of 'awkward' or 'caricatural' scenes, in particular the gallery opening. They slightly resented the in-joke of Kassovitz inserting his father and Julie Mauduech (the lead actress in *Métisse*) as cameos – especially as the joke is rather clumsily underlined: Mauduech says to Hubert, 'Haven't we met before?', and at the end of that sequence, when Vinz and Hubert violently smash property, the Peter Kassovitz character comments on 'the *banlieue* malaise'. But they also resented what they felt to be a caricatural note in the three heroes' behaviour, which Kassovitz defended however, by insisting that 'this scene is essential. Without it my trio is too sympathetic. With it I can show they are also capable of being "little jerks".'[54] One or two reviewers also felt that the ending was too contrived or derivative (of Tarantino, John Woo or Scorsese). But more serious, and more revealing, dissensions hint at areas of ambivalence in the film – areas over which, interestingly, Kassovitz contradicts himself in his responses. This relates, first, to *La Haine*'s (and Kassovitz's) relation to the social problem depicted and, on a more personal level, his 'right' to represent a milieu that is not naturally his; secondly, to his attitude towards the police; and, thirdly, to his 'recuperation' by the media.

Monique Pantel, a reviewer in *France-Soir*, was the first to pose a question that came to be asked frequently: 'How can you show life on the *cités* when you do not come from that milieu?' Aurélien Ferenczi in *InfoMatin* was even more direct: 'What right do you have to talk about the *banlieues*?'[55] Kassovitz replied: 'Yes, I know I am not from the *banlieue*. I knew I would be in trouble because of that',[56] and defended himself usually along the lines that he had 'lots of friends, some of whom come from the *banlieue*'[57] and that 'Vincent Cassel and I did not grow up in the *banlieue*, but we know its language',[58] He also said: 'Among my friends, we all talk like that!',[59] and, on an even more personal note, 'I come from an intellectual rather than bourgeois milieu. My father is a filmmaker, but he is no Stephen Spielberg, my mother is an editor.'[60] Beyond Kassovitz's personal background, this type of questioning and his answers echo the ambiguities (discussed in Chapter 1 and 2) over the status of La Haine as a 'social' or 'political' film – even if few go as far as Jean-François Richet in accusing La Haine of being 'science fiction'.[61] Scanning the numerous interviews, we see at times Kassovitz claiming his film as squarely 'social', and at others playing this dimension down. Although he makes statements such as: '[T]his is not an anodyne film. It speaks of serious social problems',[62] more frequently he goes the other way: 'I am neither a politician nor a sociologist. I did not want to make something boring, even if La Haine talks about problems which concern me';[63] or: 'I admire Ken Loach because he gave a voice to people who don't normally have it. But it does not stop me from making my film attractive.'[64] To the question: 'Does La Haine tell the truth about the cités?' he vehemently replies, 'No, absolutely not!'[65] Later, in one of the 'making of' documentaries, to the question: 'What do you have in common with your characters?' Kassovitz replies, 'Nothing.'[66]

Another, though smaller, area of contention that emerges from the reviews is that of the film's attitude to the police. As we saw at the beginning of this chapter, the film was immediately and very publicly perceived as anti-police by policemen themselves, and several critics saw it as both 'anti-L627' (Tavernier's 1997 film about the police) and 'a pamphlet against the Pasqua laws'.[67] Here too, and particularly in response to criticism, Kassovitz wavered, at times stating that 'La Haine is a film against cops and I wanted it to be understood as such',[68] or 'the film expresses the cités' hatred towards the cops';[69] at other times claiming, more diplomatically, 'La Haine is not a film against the cops. It is against the police system',[70] or, to take another quote among many, 'La Haine is a film about the bavures of the police'.[71] Both in relation to the representation of the fracture sociale and of the police, these areas of slippage correspond to ambivalences in the film text itself. These are, interestingly, picked up also in some of the comments on the CD of rap music commissioned by Kassovitz to accompany the release of the film. While Steve Cannon sees the success of La Haine and this rap album as further cementing hip-hop's presence in mainstream culture,[72] one group featured on the CD, Ministère Amer, claims: 'La Haine does not depict a reality, it is not a film about the banlieue, but the point of view of one filmmaker.'[73] The review of the CD in Les Inrockuptibles also notes the absence of 'radical' bands such as Supreme NTM from the selection, finding it far too consensual and ideologically vague: 'Stuck between the film script and their own political uncertainties, they give the impression of not knowing where they are going. [There is in the songs] too much ideological vagueness, half-baked theories and a Manichean "poetry of the riots".[74] That being said, I must reiterate that these ambivalences – which I have, of necessity emphasised by teasing them out – are small exceptions to the deluge of praise the film otherwise received.

Finally, the last and perhaps most important dissonance is Kassovitz's anxiety in relation to his film being 'recuperated' by the media. Immediately after *La Haine* was selected for Cannes, he told *France-Soir*: 'I want at all costs to avoid a fashion effect and recuperation by the media.'[75] To a *Télérama* journalist who asked: 'Isn't Cannes a strange place to show such a film?' Kassovitz replied, 'I am pleased to be hobknobbing with Ken Loach and [Emir] Kusturica … [but appalled that] fancy people tell me that they find the film "amazing, very true". I thought I would shock them more. Unfortunately I did not.'[76] To *Libération* he went further: 'I want my film to be seen. But I don't want to prostitute myself or for others to prostitute themselves to me. To be on the cover of *Première* is good for the film, but it also works against it. […] Everyone is looking for the new Luc Besson, the new Cyril Collard, in terms of media and money. It is demagogy. […] I was asked to launch a line of *La Haine* clothes for the Monoprix chain store. There is a real problem here.'[77] Naturally the film's producer, Christophe Rossignon, was more measured in his dislike of the media 'recuperation' of *La Haine*: 'The media coverage of the film went beyond anything we anticipated … but the film became a *phénomène de société* to the detriment of its filmic interest.' This may be true, though critics hardly ignored stylistic issues. But Kassovitz's reaction to his lionisation by the media and dislike of merchandising also tells us something else. While it is another symptom of ideological ambivalence in the film, it is also part of the traditional dislike on the part of French auteurs for the promotional aspect of filmmaking, seen as degrading after-sale service. As we shall see, Kassovitz appears to have worked more enthusiastically for the sale of his film in the United States, where more vigorous marketing is the norm, but also where the auteur discourse and its contempt for the industry holds less sway.

Away from these immediate contemporary reactions, *La Haine* has continued to elicit critical interest in France, mostly as part of the *jeune cinéma français* (see Chapter 1) and, more precisely, the *cinéma de banlieue* 'movement'. René Prédal even credits *La Haine* with provoking 'a more general interest in social context, leading filmmakers to root their sentimental and psychological stories in professional and regional realities'[78] – a point I will return to at the end of this chapter.

International reception

La Haine's positive reception in France was matched abroad, where it was specifically received as a welcome departure from the kind of French films normally distributed internationally. It won the 1995 European film award for 'best young film', the Golden Alexander at the 1995 Thessaloniki Film Festival, and in the 1997 the FCCA (Film Critics Circle of Australia) award, while director of photography Pierre Aïm was awarded the 'golden frog' at the Camerimage awards. The impact of *La Haine* in France, as well as these further awards, led to an active promotional campaign. Kassovitz and his three lead actors travelled to many countries, including Japan, the United Kingdom and the United States (the last two of which will be the focus of my attention here). In the United States and the United Kingdom, *La Haine* became a cult film with young audiences, overcoming the handicap of being black and white and with subtitles – features that would normally have positioned it as an 'art film' targeting an older audience. The subtitles presented special difficulties, given the copious slang; they were resolved, as is often the case, by recourse to Americanisms and other cultural translations, or cultural imperialism, depending on one's point of view (which some British reviewers – and viewers! – resented). Some may be legitimate, such as replacing Darty with Wallmart, or Malik Oussekine with Rodney King (the young Afro-American brutalised by the Los Angeles police) and Les Schtroumpfs with Donald Duck. There are also truly untranslatable jokes: translating Saïd's limerick-style 'le pénis de Le Pen à peine il se hisse', literally, as 'Le Pen's penis can hardly get up' does not do justice to a comic but also literary obscenity. However, the use of other American terms, such as Astérix becoming Snoopy and Obélix Charlie Brown, 'Kro' (for Kronenbourg) 'Bud' (Budweiser), 'pote' (mate) 'Home boy', 'Down with Le Pen' 'Fuck Nazis,' and 'Disneyland' 'Euro-Disney', are more dubious in their erasing of Frenchness. As Jonathan Romney put it, given the importance of American culture in the film, it is both 'oddly appropriate and something of a disaster that the subtitles Americanise the dialogue so completely'.[79] Adam Mars-Jones was more annoyed, pointing out: 'When you consider that France has fought a real battle against the Americanisation of films, it's ludicrous that the subtitles of *La Haine* should surrender so abjectly.'[80] Some of these excesses have been corrected in the subtitles of a 2004 British DVD release.[81]

In the United Kingdom, *La Haine* first made an impression in June 1995, when *The Guardian*[82] reported the investigation of the link between the film and the Noisy-le-Grand riots (discussed above). The film came out on 17 November 1995 (following a screening at the London Film Festival), generating abundant press coverage. Kassovitz was everywhere seen as authentic and talented, and the vigour and stylishness of the film were praised; but the real focus of reviewers was the 'hard-hitting' novelty and 'truth' value of the topic; 'shock waves from the suburbs'[83] and 'a wonderful wake-up call'[84] were two typical expressions among many. Most reviewers were at pains to describe the special qualities of the French *banlieue* and place the film in an international context. As in France, it was compared to black films ('A kind of Parisian *Boyz 'N the Hood*'),[85] but also to two other 1995 British and American films about troubled youth, *Trainspotting* (Danny Boyle) and *Kids* (Larry Clark). More generally, it was also linked to the 'Generation X' movies. Above all, the contrast with the French cinema familiar to British audiences was welcomed: 'Not another of those genteel pieces in which Emmanuelle Béart fiddles while Daniel Auteuil smoulders';[86] 'A Molotov cocktail through the sedate window front of modern French cinema';[87] 'A massive depth charge to the complacency of French cinema.'[88] A few years later an article about the *jeune cinéma français* linked *La Haine* to films such as *Seul contre tous* (Gaspar Noé, 1996), *Clubbed to Death* (Yolande Zauberman, 1996) and *Dobermann* (Jan Kounen, 1997) in terms of their 'in your-visage violence'.[89] Thus, generally, the film was seen as innovative and socially relevant, including in terms of its violence. Criticism was muted; only a few interviewers complained about the team's uncooperative attitude. *The Daily Telegraph* journalist noted of the director and his lead actors, 'They're exhausted, bored and slightly petulant; Mathieu Kassovitz plays with his mobile throughout the interview',[90] while Tom Charity in *Time Out* charted Kassovitz's sullen attitude and his annoyed outburst that '[M]y job is not to give interviews.'[91]

Kassovitz was noticeably more cooperative in the United States, where Jodie Foster endorsed the film and they 'worked together on its intense promotion'.[92] Foster took a leading role, 'supervising promotional leaflets, the number of television ads and exhibition channels. She accepted to see journalists only with Kassovitz: thus they covered the political and specialised (rap music) radio stations, campus audiences, the art media, MTV as well as PBS.'[93] Foster's sponsorship was part of a campaign by American film personalities to help independent and potentially 'difficult' foreign films find an audience in the United States. In the case of *La Haine*, this seems to have paid off: 'Contrary to the received dogma in American film distribution, nobody had problems in watching a film in black and white and reading subtitles.'[94] When the film opened on 9 February 1996 it was initially shown in one cinema in New York, where it did very well, taking over $20,000 in the first three days.[95] Subsequently, it was shown across the country. American reviewers registered similar reactions to their British counterparts, noting the 'burning immediacy'[96] of the film's topic and Kassovitz's 'mature tone and narrative cohesion'.[97] There was, however, a hint of chauvinistic condescending: J. Hoberman in *The Village Voice* in an otherwise perceptive review sardonically pointed out that the film's references to American culture were 'an exotic sort of déjà vu. Like, where would the rest of the world be without Us?'[98] And if Rogert Ebert in *The Chicago Sun-Times* rather elegantly stated that the 'characters inhabit a world where much of the cultural furniture has been imported from America' and mused that '[P]erhaps they like US culture because it is not French, and they do not feel very French, either',[99] others were downright patronising. Barbara Shulgasser in *The San Francisco Examiner* found it 'quaint' that the three heroes were 'still dressing pretty much like homeboys of the late '70s and early '80s, in warm-ups, rather than the baggy plaid shirts of self-respecting young thugs from East L.A. and South Chicago. They're trying to be hip but they're a little behind the times.'[100]

Discussions in the specialist Anglo-American film press and academic journals on the whole shifted away from the aesthetic agenda of many French writers. Susan Morrison in the Canadian journal *CineAction!* was something of an exception in praising Kassovitz for moving his story 'out of the more localized American black ethnic experience into the universal, an inclusionary artistic expression rather than an exclusionary one' as she proceeded to compare the film to those of Wong Kar-Wai and John Woo.[101] Otherwise, *La Haine* was placed in two overlapping interpretative frameworks. On one side, as in France, some writers approached *La Haine* in terms of the specificity of the *banlieue-film* and in terms of geography and space.[102] On the other side, the agenda was transposed to race and ethnicity, and, to a lesser extent, gender – two aspects of the film largely ignored by French writers, who on the whole merely recorded the fact that women were absent from the film. In this respect, Anglo-American studies were both more sustained (showing the strength of English-language post-colonial and gender studies) but also often more judgemental about the film. Like Jim Pines in *The Voice*,[103] Bérénice Reynaud praised the 'searing originality' of the film in terms of its ability to 'deal with the racial and ethnic mix of [its] own national landscape'.[104] Others were more critical. For Carrie Tarr, as discussed earlier, while Kassovitz's films address ethnicity, in both *La Haine* and *Métisse* 'it is the figure of the white (Jewish) male which provides the main structuring interest of the films' narratives'; *La Haine* 'structures two *Beur* youths into the narrative, only to use them in ways which deny them an active role'.[105] Others talked of 'Benetton-ad glibness'.[106] Most critical was filmmaker Karen Alexander. For her, the 'endless references to and mimicry of African-American culture [and] designer labels... dissipate the potential strength of [Kassovitz'] subject matter. [...] To filter his narrative through a transatlantic superstructure is to lose a specifically European "otherness"'. One can dispute this view of Europe as somehow untouched by global culture as romantic. On the other hand, Alexander is one of the few writers to address the issue of gender head-on. Pondering the huge success of the film, contrary to Reynaud, who argues that Kassovitz's 'aim is clearly to delimitate a territory (urban, social, symbolic, filmic) for disenfranchised young males',[107] Alexander notes the sexism in evidence in the film ('women, when seen, are either mothers or referred to as 'bitch' and 'pussy'), and suggests that 'the answer, I feel, has a lot to do with Mathieu Kassovitz being young and male', and having learned 'enough about the media as a whole to know that police brutality, urban violence and communities under siege will always get you a headline'.[108]

La Haine continues to be analysed (positively or negatively) by English-speaking academic writers in terms of its representation of the *banlieue*, the *fracture sociale* and ethnicity; for instance Jill Forbes' chapter in her co-edited book *European Cinema* discusses *La Haine* as a '*zeitgeist* film'.[109] In an interesting twist, it even figures as the only French film out of ten recommended by a group of British Muslims polled by *The Guardian*.[110] By contrast, we find startlingly different analyses in France. For instance, in a 1998 retrospective piece in *Cahiers du cinéma*, Emmanuel Burdeau claims that *La Haine* 'makes the *banlieue* finally watchable', but 'effectively says nothing decisive or interesting about [it] (and is careful not to be informative about what goes on there)'.[111] In a nutshell, we have a perfect illustration both of the reasons for the positive consensus around the film and of the continued split in critical practice: towards aesthetics on the French side, and sociocultural issues in the Anglo-American world.

A lucky break: life after *La Haine*

For all those involved, *La Haine* was a lucky break, leading to substantial careers – though more substantial for some than others. In 1995 Kassovitz said of the future: 'My next film will be about the role of media. The responsibility of TF1 [the main privatised television channel] will be judged in 10 years' time. We will be dealing with young people who have only had images of violence and sex.'[112] *Assassin(s)*, which came out in 1997, was indeed such a film. But, by contrast with the ecstatic reception of *La Haine*, *Assassin(s)* was dealt a severe critical thrashing. *Le Figaro* dubbed it 'the most worthless film in the history of cinema'.[113] Kassovitz shrugged off this hostility with: 'Whatever I did after *La Haine* would have been criticized.'[114] This may be the case; others have plausibly spoken of a backlash 'to make Kassovitz pay for the insolent success of *La Haine*'.[115] On the other hand, it has to be said that *Assassin(s)* is gloomy and complacent – a reflection on images of male violence, yes, but also a wallowing in them. More interestingly, *Assassin(s)* reflects a return to Kassovitz's adolescent themes of (and taste for) extreme violence, which he has pursued subsequently. If Will Higbee sees *Assassin(s)* as the last instalment in a *'fracture sociale* trilogy'[116] including *Métisse* and *La Haine*, a stronger case can be made for it as a transition towards his later manner – films that have showcased spectacular displays of violence and gore, abandoning all reference to the social reality of France: 'It is not up to me to do this, at thirty-six I am too old. It does not interest me any more. It's not my life, I am not Ken Loach.'[117]

Assassin(s) was followed by *Les Rivières pourpres/The Crimson Rivers* in 2000 – a film with a budget of some FF100,000,000/$18,000,000 (remember that *La Haine* was made on FF15,000,000/$2,8000,000), and a substantial box-office success. Then in 2003 he made the Hollywood horror/thriller *Gothika*, with a budget of $40,000,000 starring Halle Berry and Penelope Cruz, which met also with substantial success in France (over 1,200,000 spectators) as well as in America.[118] Kassovitz makes no bones about his ambition to achieve the international big time through genre cinema, and he candidly calls *Gothika* 'a series of horror movie clichés'.[119] Even if the 1995 project to direct Jodie Foster's next film[120] has not (yet) borne fruit, his career plan has clearly paid off: 'I made *Les Rivières pourpres* in order to make *Gothika*, I did *Gothika* in order to do *Babylon* [*Babylon Babies*].'[121] The latter – in production at the time of writing – is a spectacular French science fiction fantasy, shot in English in Canada, with American money.

Besides filmmaking, Kassovitz has also been involved in two production companies, MNP Entreprises (which involves Rossignon) and the short-lived 1B2K (with Luc Besson and Jan Kounen), and in early 2004 he was reported as wanting to produce cartoons for children as well as scripts for video games, and to be involved in an Imax project.[122] He has meanwhile, pursued a flourishing career as an actor. His most prominent parts since *La Haine* have been the conman who invents a Resistance past in *Un héros très discret* (1996), Nino Quincampoix in the hit romantic comedy *Le Fabuleux destin d'Amélie Poulain* (2001), a success which also launched his career as a model for the Lancôme perfume 'Miracle', and as a Catholic priest who defied the Vatican's anti-Semitic policies during the war in *Amen* (2002).

La Haine likewise propelled Vincent Cassel to stardom. In the press coverage and interviews feting the success of the three lead actors, Cassel was immediately singled out.[123] His subsequent acting roles have included romantic parts in films such as *Adultère mode d'emploi* (Christine Pascal, 1995) and *L'Appartement* (Gilles Mimouni, 1996), but more characteristic of his tough-guy persona are his parts in *Le Pacte des loups* (Christophe

Premiere of re-release of *La Haine*, The Screen on the Green cinema, London,
17 August 2004

Gans, 2001), *Les Rivières pourpres* and *Sur mes lèvres* (Jacques Audiard, 2001), in which he brilliantly plays an almost autistic hoodlum, as well as the extremely violent *Irréversible* (Gaspar Noé, 2002) – each of which prolongs a line begun in *La Haine*.

Taghmaoui and Koundé, since *La Haine*, have done well but, predictably, much less so than Cassel. As *Le Journal du Dimanche* puts it, they both inhabit 'the narrow niche of French actors "of colour"';[124] and Cassel has readily admitted that 'the injustice in relation to Saïd and Hubert is obvious: "I am white", my name is Cassel, we are in France, and it will always be easier for me than for them.'[125] Taghmaoui, in fact, has had a fairly busy international career since *La Haine*, but his parts have tended towards the stereotypical 'Arab' – for instance, in *Hideous Kinky* (Gillies MacKinnon, 1998), *Room to Rent* (Khalid Al-Haggar, 2000) and *The Good Thief* (Neil Jordan, 2002). As for Koundé, he was sent a string of proposals, but only in 'cliché roles of dealers and boxers, which [he] turned down'.[126] He has, however, worked in Peter Brook's prestigious troupe at Les Bouffes du Nord theatre, appeared in minor French film roles and starred in the Senegalese film *Ndeysaan* (Mansour Sora Wade, 2002). Even if, as discussed in Chapter 1, the situation for non-white actors is changing, progress is slow, as the examples above indicate. Perhaps the greatest irony is provided by Kassovitz's adaptation of Jean-Christophe Grangé's thriller for *Les Rivières pourpres*. The film erases the fact that one of the two main characters in the novel is a young *beur* cop, a character who would have provided a great opportunity for a non-stereotypical role for a *beur* actor (if not necessarily Taghmaoui). Kassovitz made the cop white and gave the part to ... Vincent Cassel.

Conclusion

La Haine was perceived in 1995 as both harbinger and epitome of the *film de banlieue,* as well as a welcome breath of fresh air in French cinema. Although at the time of its release, writers such as Myrto Konstantarakos believed that 'the importance of these films lies principally with the creation of a new genre',[127] ten years later it is clear that this has not happened. While *La Haine* was too original and too hybrid to lead to a 'genre', it is also the case that Kassovitz, like fellow *beur* and *banlieue* filmmakers Merzak Allouache, Malik Chibane and Jean-François Richet among others, has branched out towards mainstream cinema. In the same way as *cinéma beur* as a movement belongs to the 1980s, the *film de banlieue* can be seen as a 'moment' in 1990s French cinema, of which *La Haine* was the best, most successful but also most idiosyncratic example.

In other respects *La Haine* was not a flash in the pan. The film's reputation has endured and grown. At present several VHS and at least four DVD versions exist in France and the United Kingdom. Its status as a classic text is confirmed by the very existence of this book of course, but also by two shorter students' guides, published in Belgium in 1996 (written by Michel Condé) and in the United Kingdom in 2000 (written by Roy Stafford).[128] Similarly, despite its scantiness in the film, music has continued to produce spin-offs beyond the French rap CD inspired by the film: on 21 June 2002, as part of David Bowie's 'Meltdown 2002', Asian Dub Foundation (ADF) performed a live score to a screening of the film in the Royal Festival Hall, London; other concerts followed, notably in Brussels, and ADF's 2004 album 'Enemy of the Enemy' features a track called '*La Haine*', themed after the film. At the time of writing the film was re-released in the United Kingdom, in the presence of the director, for its '10th anniversary' (odd, since it was actually its ninth...). As acknowledged by Kassovitz in the quote that opens this chapter, *La Haine* has totally dominated his life and career, despite often considerable achievements subsequently. On university film courses, the film is sure to generate animated, even passionate discussion.

A 'cool' cultural aura, a young director, young and attractive stars and a youth audience (including a strong campus following), humour, violence, street cred: *La Haine* has all the hallmarks of a cult film. But it also has social relevance, stylistic virtuosity, and the ability to speak both of its own country and to transcend its national borders – in other words, the qualifications for classicism. Able to elicit passion as well as provoke thought, *La Haine* is both a cult movie and a classic film.

Notes

1   'Douze mois de haine', *Studio Magazine*, special issue 'L'Année Cinéma', 1995, p. 104.
2   Ibid., p. 104.
3   Coppermann, *Les Echos*, 31 May 1995.
4   Ferenczi, *InfoMatin*, 29 May 1995.
5   Seguret, *Libération*, 29 May 1995.
6   'Douze mois de haine', p. 105.
7   J.D., 'interview du fanzine *Steadycam*'.
8   This can be seen on the Canal+ DVD, *La Haine*, 2001.
9   'Douze mois de haine', p. 103.
10 The soundtrack of the film (which includes music from *Métisse*) had its release delayed by the clearing of rights to Bob Marley's 'Burnin' and Lootin'' and Isaac Hayes' *That Loving Feeling*, so it was not available when the film came out. See Brown, Colin, 'Harmony and discord', *Screen International*, 1 December 1995, pp. 10–12.

11 *Ciné-Passions*, p. 102.
12 Cited in enquiry by Marie-Elisabeth Rouchy (with Isabelle Danel and Bernard Génin), *Télérama*, 28 June 1995.
13 Le Leurch, Vincent, *Télérama*, 28 June 1995.
14 Ibid.
15 Cited in Celmar, R. and Fufresne, David, *Libération*, 5 June 1995.
16 Ibid.
17 Cited in Kerchouche, Dalila, 'Un film à tout casser', *L'Express*, 15 June 1995, p. 70.
18 Cited in enquiry by Marie-Elisabeth Rouchy (with Isabelle Danel and Bernard Génin), *Télérama*, 28 June 1995.
19 Wenz-Dumas, François, 'Nuit bleue très minutée à Noisy-le-Grand', *Libération*, 10 June 1995.
20 In particular, Dubet, François and Lapeyronnie, Didier, *Les Quartiers de l'exil*. Paris, Éditions de Seuil, 1992.
21 Dubet, François, in C. Gilbert, 'Les miroirs de la haine', *L'Express*, 15 June 1995, p. 68.
22 'Douze mois de haine', p. 105.
23 *Le Figaro magazine*, 10 June 1996.
24 Riou, *Le Nouvel Observateur*, 25 May 1995.
25 Cassel, Jean-Pierre, *France-Soir*, 27 May 1995.
26 Ferenczi, Aurélien, *InfoMatin*, 29 May 1995.
27 Pantel, Interview with Mathieu Kassovitz.
28 Riou, *Le Nouvel Observateur*, 25 May 1995.
29 Chemineau, Sophie, *La Tribune Desfossés*, 31 May 1995.
30 *L'Express*, 11 May 1995.
31 Riou, *Le Nouvel Observateur*, 25 May 1995.
32 Coppermann, *Les Echos*, 31 May 1995.
33 Ferenczi, *InfoMatin*, 31 May 1995.
34 Murat, Pierre, *Télérama*, 31 May 1995.
35 Ferenczi, *InfoMatin*, 31 May 1995.
36 De Bruyn, Olivier, *Les Inrockuptibles*, 31 May 1995.
37 Ferenczi, *InfoMatin*, 29 May 1995.
38 Riou, *Le Nouvel Observateur*, 25 May 1995.
39 Seguret, *Libération*, 29 May 1995.
40 J.D., 'interview du fanzine *Steadycam*'.
41 *Cahiers du cinéma*, June 1995, pp. 32–35.
42 *Positif*, June 1995, pp 4–13.
43 Jousse, Thierry, 'Prose combat', *Cahiers du cinéma*, June 1995, pp. 32–35.
44 Sibony, Daniel, 'Exclusion intrinsèque: À propos de *La Haine*', *Cahiers du cinéma*, July–August 1995, pp. 30–31, pp. 183–203.
45 Tobin, Yann, 'État des (ban)lieues', *Positif*, September 1995, p. 28.
46 Mongin, 'Regarde-les tomber', pp. 172–186.
47 *Cahiers du cinéma*, June 1995, pp. 34–35.
48 *Positif*, 412, June 1995, p. 6
49 Valletoux, Thierry, 'Kassovitz en plein cauchemar', *Studio Magazine*, September 1994, p. 117.
50 Parent, Denis, '*La Haine*', *Studio Magazine*, June 1995, p. 9.
51 *Le Film Français*, 3 November 1995.

52 Tranchant, *Le Figaro*, 27 May 1995.
53 Murat, *Télérama*, 31 May 1995.
54 Rémy, *Télérama*, interview with Mathieu Kassovitz.
55 Ferenczi, *InfoMatin*, 31 May 1995.
56 Rémy, interview with Mathieu Kassovitz.
57 Pantel, interview with Mathieu Kassovitz.
58 Rémy, interview with Mathieu Kassovitz.
59 'Interview with Mathieu Kassovitz', p. 193.
60 Ferenczi, *InfoMatin*, 31 May 1995.
61 Richet, Jean-François, (director of the Marxist *banlieue-film État des lieux*), quoted in J.D., 'interview du fanzine *Steadycam*'.
62 Tranchant, *Le Figaro*, 27 May 1995.
63 Pantel, *France-Soir*, interview with Mathieu Kassovitz.
64 Tranchant, *Le Figaro*, 27 May 1995.
65 Ferenczi, *InfoMatin*, 31 May 1995.
66 Canal+ DVD, *La Haine*, 2001.
67 Ferenczi, *InfoMatin*, 29 May 1995 (see Chapter 1 for a discussion of the Pasqua laws).
68 Seguret, *Libération*, 29 May 1995.
69 *L'Express*, 11 May 1995.
70 Levieux, *L'Humanité*, 29 May 1995.
71 Rémy, interview with Mathieu Kassovitz.
72 Cannon, 'Paname City rapping', p. 160.
73 *Les Inrockuptibles*, 31 May 1995.
74 Ibid.
75 Pantel, interview with Mathieu Kassovitz.
76 Rémy, interview with Mathieu Kassovitz.
77 Boulay and Colmant, *Libération*, 31 May 1995.
78 Prédal, *Le Jeune Cinéma français*, p. 117.
79 Romney, Jonathan, '*La Haine (Hate)*', in J. Romney, *Short Orders: Film Writing*. London, Serpent's Tail, 1997, p. 197.
80 Mars-Jones, Adam, '*La Haine*', *The Independent*, 16 November 1995, pp. 10–11.
81 DVD, Optimum Releasing *La Haine*, 2004.
82 Duval Smith, Alex, 'When the cinema becomes la vérité', *The Guardian*, 23 June 1995, pp. 20–21.
83 *The Daily Telegraph*, 11 November 1995, p. 15.
84 *The Times*, 16 November 1995, p. 35.
85 'The business', *Sight and Sound*, 5, (9), 1995, p. 4.
86 *The Evening Standard Magazine*, 27 October 1995, p. 45.
87 *The Independent on Sunday*, 19 November 1995, p. 16
88 Romney, '*La Haine (Hate)*', p. 198.
89 Spencer, Liese, *The Independent*, 14 January 1999.
90 Reid, Vicki, *The Daily Telegraph*, 11 November 1995.
91 Charity, interview with Mathieu Kassovitz.
92 Béhar, Henri, *Le Monde*, 15 February 1996. See also 'Pourquoi Jodie Foster parraine *La Haine*', *Le Film Français*, 10 November 1995, p. 23.
93 Béhar, *Le Monde*, 15 February 1996.
94 Ibid.
95 Mousselard, Olivier-Pascal, *La Tribune Desfossés*, 14 February 1996.

96 Blackburn, Olly, *Interview*, 26, (3), 1996, p. 52.
97 Nesselson, Lisa, *Variety*, 29 June 1995.
98 Hoberman, J. 'Alien nations', *The Village Voice*, 13 February 1996.
99 Ebert, *The Chicago Sun-Times*, 4 April 1996.
100 Shulgasser, Barbara, *The San Francisco Examiner*, 5 April 1996.
101 Morrison, Susan, '*La Haine, Fallen Angels*, and some thoughts on Scorsese's Children', *CineAction!*, December 1995.
102 See, in particular: Reader, 'After the riot', pp. 12–14; Higbee, 'Screening the "other" Paris', pp. 197–208; Fielder, 'Poaching on public space'; Konstantarakos, 'Which mapping of the city?'.
103 Pines, Jim, quoted in *The Voice*, 10 October 1995, pp. 25–26.
104 Reynaud, Bérénice, 'Le "hood"', *Film Comment*, 32, (2), 1996, p. 54.
105 Tarr, 'Ethnicity and identity in *Métisse* and *La Haine*'.
106 'GM', *Sight and Sound*, 2, (4), p. 63.
107 Reynaud, 'Le "hood"', p. 55.
108 Alexander, '*La Haine*', pp. 42–47.
109 Forbes, Jill, '*La Haine*', in J. Forbes and S. Street (eds), *European Cinema, An Introduction*. London, Palgrave, 2000, p. 171.
110 Cited in Malcolm, Derek, 'The greatest stories ever told?', *The Guardian*, 13 April 1996, p. 30.
111 Burdeau, Emmanuel, '68/98, retours et détours', *Cahiers du cinéma*, special issue 'cinéma 1968', 1998, p. 44.
112 Rémy, interview with Mathieu Kassovitz.
113 Quoted on the French VHS of *Assassin(s)*, Canal+, 1997.
114 J.D., 'interview du fanzine *Steadycam*'.
115 Goudet, Stéphane, in M. Marie (ed.), *Le jeune cinéma français*, p. 119.
116 Higbee, Will, paper presented at the conference on 'Studies in French Cinema', French Institute, London, 16 April 2004.
117 Apiou, Virginie, *Synopsis*, 29, January/February 2004, p. 24.
118 For a budget of US$ 40m – now relatively modest by US standards – and US$ 25m for marketing, worldwide gross was US$ 141m, a decent success.
119 Apiou, interview with Mathieu Kassovitz, p. 24.
120 *Première*, December 1995, p. 85.
121 Apiou, interview with Mathieu Kassovitz, p. 23.
122 Ibid., p. 23.
123 For instance a long interview in *Studio Magazine*, July–August 1995.
124 Campion, Alexis, *Le Journal du Dimanche*, 12 November 1995.
125 *Télérama*, 1996, pp. 36–38.
126 Campion, *Le Journal du Dimanche*, 12 November 1995.
127 Konstantarakos, 'Which mapping of the city?', p. 169.
128 Details of these books can be found in the bibliography. No doubt other works exist in languages other than French and English.

Appendix 1: Credits

Crew

Director: Mathieu Kassovitz; Production: Les Productions Lazennec, in coproduction with Le Studio Canal+/La Sept Cinema/Kasso Inc. Productions, with assistance from Sofica Cofimage 6 & Studio Images, with the participation of Canal+; Producer: Christophe Rossignon; Associate producers: Adeline Lecallier, Alain Rocca; Line producer: Gilles Sacuto; Unit production manager: Sophie Quiédeville; Assistant: Clémentine Thomas; Production administrator: Thierry Artur; Production secretary: Laure Darie; Production trainees: Karine Tuchming, Thierry Pichard, Sylvain Chatenoud, Guillaume Favreau; Scriptwriter: Mathieu Kassovitz; Director of photography: Pierre Aïm
Camera operator: Georges Diane; Assistant camera operators: Marie Spencer, Axel Cosnefroy, Hervé Lodé; Steadicam operator: Jacques Monge; Editors: Mathieu Kassovitz, Scott Stevenson; Assistant editor: Stratos Gabrielidis; First assistant director: Eric Pujol; Second assistant director: Ludovic Bernard; Trainee assistant director: François Pujol; Art director: Giuseppe Ponturo; Assistant: Richard Guille; Costumes: Virginie Montel; Assistant: Nathalie Chemouny; Make-up: Sophie Benaiche; Prop master: Jean-Louis Laher; Trainee decorator: Jean-Michel Bar; Sound: Vincent Tulli; Sound mixer: Dominique Dalmasso; Assistant: Dominique Vieillard; Sound recordists: Bruno Cottance, Valérie Trouette; Sound re-recordists: Patrice Severac, Frédéric Mays; Sound effects: Nicolas Becker; Assistant: Assia Dnednia; Boom operator: Emmanuel Ughetto; Trainee: Laure Monrreal; Visual effects: Antoine Simkine; Special effects: Pierre Foury; Special effect assistants: Pascal Fauvelle, Benoît Squizzato, Olivier Zenenski; Stunt coordinator: Philippe Guégan; Stuntmen: Bernard Chevreuil, Gilles Conseil, Mohamed Enahal, Christian Hening, Abdel Halim, Patrick Medioni, Pascal Guégan
Location manager: Abdelnabi Krouchi; Gaffer: Mikael Monod; Electricians: Christian Vicq, Frédéric Loustalot, Philippe Gibier; Chief technicians: Vincent Blasco, Alex Bugel; Chief builder: Alain Darthou; Chief painter: Cyrille Perron; Carpenters: Nicolas Denis, Jérôme Fortier, Bruno Lefevre, Frédéric Perron; Caterers: Thierry Six, Emmanuel Blouin; Post-production: Sylvie Randonneix; Casting: Jean-Claude Flamand; Assistant: Arash Mansour; Continuity: Nathalie Vierny; Video archive research: Armelle Bayle; Still photographers: Guy Ferrandis, Jean-Claude Lother; Press office: François Guerrar; International sales: Le Studio Canal+

Running time: 1h 35 minutes
Production format: 35mm

Negative and positive film: Kodak (colour, printed black and white)
Projection format: 1:85.1
Sound format: Dolby stereo digital

Pre-credit text: Ce film est dédié à ceux disparus pendant sa fabrication... (This film is dedicated to those who disappeared while it was being made...).

Post-credit text: Toute resemblance avec des événements ou personnes existant ou ayant existé ne serait que purement fortuite et indépendante de la volonté des auteurs (Any similarity with events or persons existing or having existed would be purely fortuitous and beyond the will of the authors).

Cast

Vincent Cassel: Vinz; Hubert Koundé: Hubert; Saïd Taghmaoui: Saïd
Karim Belkhadra Samir (*beur* plainclothes policeman in *cité*); Édouard Montoute: Darty; François Levantal: Astérix; Solo Dicko: Santo; Marc Duret: Inspector 'Notre-Dame' (plainclothes policeman in *cité*); Héloïse Rauth: Sarah, Vinz's sister; Rywka Wajsbrot: Vinz's grandmother; Tadek Lokcinski: old man in toilets; Choukri Gabteni: Nordine, Saïd's brother; Nabil Ben Mhamed: Young boy who tells story in *cité*; Félicité Wouassi: Hubert's mother; Fatou Thioune: Hubert's sister; Philippe Nahon: Police chief in *cité* (roof scene); Sébastien Tavel: young hospital police officer; François Toumarkine: chief hospital police officer; José-Philippe Dalmat: hospital police officer no. 1; Zinedine Soualem: plainclothes police officer in Paris no. 1; Bernie Bonvoisin: plainclothes police officer in Paris no. 2; Cyril Ancelin: plainclothes police officer in Paris no. 3; Julie Mauduech: woman in art gallery; Karin Viard: woman in art gallery; Peter Kassovitz: Head of art gallery; Vincent Lindon: 'really' drunken man; Christophe Rossignon: taxi driver; Mathieu Kassovitz: young skinhead; Anthony Souter: skinhead; Florent Lavandeira: Skinhead; Teddy Marques: skinhead; Samir Khelif: skinhead; Eric Pujol: assistant policeman in *cité*; Patrick Médioni: CRS in *cité* cellar; Joseph Momo: 'ordinary man' (neighbour in *cité*); Laurent Labasse: cook on roof in *cité*; Benoît Magimel: Benoît; Médard Niang: Médard; Arash Mansour: Arash; Abdel-Moulah Boujdouni: Hubert's drugs customer; JiBi: youth in *cité*; Thang Long: Vietnamese grocer; Cut Killer: DJ; Sabrina Houicha: Saïd's sister; Sandor Weltmann: Vinz mirror image (in bathroom scene); Virginie Montel: beggar in Métro; Olga Abrego: Vinz's aunt; Mathilde Vitry: Journalist; Christian Moro: TV journalist; Andrée Damant: concierge; Astérix Marcel Marondo: club bouncer; Abdel Ahmed Ghili: Abdel

Music/song extracts

'Burnin' and Lootin', by and performed by Bob Marley
'That Loving Feeling', by Tony Joe White, performed by Isaac Hayes
'More Bounce to the Ounce', by Roger Troutman, performed by Zapp and Roger
'Mon esprit part en couille', by Weedy and Expression Direkt, performed by Expression Direkt
'DJ Skud Interlude', by and performed by Cut Killer
'Wedding Songs Medley', by Etan Massuri
'Funk Funk', by Larry Blackmon, performed by Cameo Song

'Tak Hedat', by and performed by Tak Fari Nas

'Outstanding', by and performed by The Gap Band

'Loufou Lakari', by and performed by Mabiala and Lonningisa

'The Beat Goes On', by Burks, Carter, Lee, Sherrer, Smith, performed by Ripple

'Nsangu Nsangu', by and performed by Klay M

'Ellens Gesang III' ('Ave Maria'), by Franz Schubert, performed by Christa Ludwig and Irwin Cage

'Hard Core', by and performed by Solo

'Groove Holmes', 'Ricky's Theme', by M. Diamond, A. Yauch, A Horowitz, M. Nishita, E. Bobo, performed by The Beastie Boys

'Eugene's Lament', by M. Diamond, A. Yauch, A Horowitz, M. Nishita, performed by The Beastie Boys

Music from the cartoon series 'Les Schtroumpfs', by W. Hanna, J. Barbera, H. J. Curtin

Music from the television series 'Chapi Chapo', by François de Roubaix

Appendix 2: Scene breakdown

Times in bold are the running time of the film (taken from the 2001 Canal+ DVD); times in italics are those that appear in the film. This breakdown is established according to the internal coherence of the sequences, and does not necessarily correspond to DVD chapters.

Part I: The *Cité*

00:00:00 – Sequence 1: Credits; montage of riot scenes
Credits intercut with documentary scenes of riots over a Bob Marley song. A picture of earth explodes when a grenade is thrown at it. Hubert's voice-over tells a story.

00:05:09 – Sequence 2: Meeting Saïd, Vinz and Hubert
[*10:30*] Presentation of the heroes, Saïd, Vinz and Hubert. We are introduced to Vinz's family and see Hubert dealing drugs in the streets.

00:14:14 – Sequence 3: The rooftop
Saïd, Vinz and Hubert meet Saïd's brother and other local boys hanging out on a rooftop; we hear that a cop lost his gun during the riots. The party is broken up by the police.

00:18:56 – Sequence 4: Hanging around; Darty; telling stories
[*12:43*] Saïd, Vinz and Hubert hang around. They respond aggressively to TV reporters. They visit Darty, a local fence. [*14:12*] A boy tells them a candid camera story.

00:25:55 – Sequence 5: The gun
Vinz shows the other two that he has the gun lost by the cop.

00:27:50 – Sequence 6: The hospital; the police station
[*15:57*] Saïd, Vinz and Hubert try to visit Abdel in hospital; they create trouble when they are turned away. Saïd is arrested. Vinz and Hubert fetch him at the police station, where he is released by Samir. They argue because Vinz has kept the gun.

00:33:58 – Sequence 7: Hubert at home; Vinz and Saïd at the grocer
Hubert goes home to his mother and sister. Vinz has a row with the Vietnamese grocer. Hubert parcels out drugs and smokes while listening to music.

00:38:37 – Sequence 8: The DJ; Saïd's haircut; break-dancing
A DJ mixes rap music with Edith Piaf; Vinz 'sees' a cow and cuts Saïd's hair. [*17:04*] They meet Saïd's sister and find Hubert again; they all watch young men break-dancing.

00:45:18 – Sequence 9: Fighting in the *cité*
A fight breaks out in the *cité* as Abdel's brother fires at policemen; CRS police intervene and the young men escape through cellars; Hubert knocks out a CRS man. Vinz, Saïd and Hubert go to Paris by train.

Part II: Paris

00:47:44 – Sequence 10: The old man in the toilets
Saïd, Vinz and Hubert are in Paris. [*18:22*] In the toilets of a café, an old man tells them a story about Jewish deportation in Siberia. They rebuff a woman beggar in the Métro.

00:54:27 – Sequence 11: Astérix
Vinz, Saïd and Hubert visit 'Astérix', who owes Saïd money. Vinz starts fighting with Astérix and they leave the flat in a hurry.

01:01:32 – Sequence 12: The police station; the cinema
Saïd and Hubert are arrested by the police outside Asterix's block of flats; Vinz escapes and goes to the cinema. [*20:17*] Saïd and Hubert are brutally assaulted by two policemen in the station while a rookie watches.

01:06:41 – Sequence 13: The boxing match; the nightclub
[*22:08*] Vinz goes to a boxing match, where he meets friends. Later they are turned away from a nightclub, and Vinz fantasises about his friend shooting the bouncer.

01:09:16 – Sequence 14: The art gallery
[*00:33*] Hubert and Saïd miss the last train home but meet again with Vinz at the station. The three gatecrash a party in an art gallery, but are thrown out when they rudely chat up two women.

01:15:39 – Sequence 15: The car; the Eiffel Tower; the poster
Despite a stolen credit card, they are unable to take a taxi. They try unsuccessfully to steal a car and are saved from the police by a friendly drunken man. They escape to a rooftop, from which they watch the Eiffel Tower. [*2:57*] Saïd sprays a poster.

01:24:14 – Sequence 16: Les Halles; Abdel's death; skinheads
In the underground shopping mall of Les Halles, they learn about Abdel's death from a giant television screen. [*04:27*] Vinz fantasises about shooting two policemen. They fight with skinheads, though Vinz refrains from shooting one of them.

Part III: Coda: Back in the *Cité*

01:30:34 – Sequence 17: The violent ending
[*06:00*] Back in the *cité*, Vinz gives up his gun to Hubert. Inspector Notre-Dame
assaults him and shoots him accidentally. [*06:01*] Hubert and Notre-Dame are
locked into a 'Mexican stand-off'. As Saïd looks on the screen goes black, and we
hear a gunshot while Hubert's voice-over finishes his story.

01:32:51 – End credits

Appendix 3: My visit to Chanteloup-les-Vignes

On a hot afternoon in August 1999, as I was finishing an essay on *La Haine* (which triggered off my interest in the film, now developed into this book), I decided to visit the estate where Mathieu Kassovitz had shot the film. There were three reasons why I wanted to do this. The first was that I was intrigued by the contradictory discourses surrounding the place (in reports, on the internet). It was not clear to me whether Chanteloup-les-Vignes was just an average, 'ordinary' estate, as Mathieu Kassovitz claimed, or whether, as some reports seemed to hint, it was one of those notorious, hellish places (*banlieues chaudes*). Secondly, and more prosaically, I wanted to take a few pictures in order to illustrate my essay.

My third reason was my own relationship to the *banlieue*. Between the ages of four and 14, I was brought up in a council block in La Courneuve, part of the 'red belt' north-east of Paris – close to the location for Jean-Luc Godard's *Deux ou trois choses que je sais d'elle* (I always get a thrill when I glimpse my old building in a shot of a petrol station near the beginning of the film). Then my parents, who had moved to La Courneuve from their parents' farms in the Vendée, realised their dream and bought a two-storey house (*pavillon*) with a garden in Villepinte, further out of Paris to the north-east, on the way to what was then not yet Charles De Gaulle airport. The house, garden and area where they still live has retained its air of semi-rurality (you can hear cocks crowing in the morning), yet over the last 30 years the proximity of the airport, the RER (Réseau Express Régional) train line, the giant shopping malls and motorways have changed the area beyond recognition. The empty land between Villepinte and the encroaching suburbs has been filled in, and waves of different habitats and immigrants have surrounded the leafy gardens and small houses of my parents' Clos Montceleux area. Brutalist 1960s tower blocks came first, followed by funkier 1970s circular blocks with scooped balconies; then, in the 1980s and 1990s, smaller estates of decreasing height, the latest version a postmodern pastiche of the kind of house my parents live in. Similarly, the white, upwardly mobile working-class inhabitants of the 1960s were joined by Vietnamese and North Africans, then black Africans, and more recently people from Eastern Europe and Sri Lanka. Next to my parents' local RER station of Sevran-

Good intentions: portraits of
great French men of arts: in
order of appearance:
Baudelaire, Hugo, Nerval,
Mallarmé, Rimbaud and
Valery on the walls of the
Chanteloup-les-Vignes

Beaudottes is the notorious eponymous estate, and most of the time youths in sports gear loiter by the station, surrounded by the flow of shoppers going to the huge Carrefour supermarket next door. People of all colours and ethnic groups mingle, usually quite peacefully.

All this is to say that I thought I knew pretty much everything there is to know about the Paris *banlieue* and felt faintly irritated by the distant, and to my mind patronising, gaze that most writing on the film adopted; material written or spoken by people who on the whole do not live in the *banlieue*, whereas – when I'm in Paris – I do! (I realise now that my reaction is similar to that of the young people quoted in the preceding section of this book.)

My long experience of the Paris *banlieue* did not, however, prepare me for Chanteloup-les-Vignes. First there is the journey. Like Vinz, Saïd and Hubert, you have to take a not very frequent train from the Gare Saint-Lazare, as Chanteloup is not on the RER. Between Saint-Lazare and Chanteloup the line offers a range of urban Parisian and suburban experiences – from the station approach (shades of Monet) to Chanteloup you run the gamut from the chic-est of Parisian quarters to grim modernist hell, and then posh leafy and hilly suburbs with tennis courts and swimming pools. On that day in August 1999, during the course of the 45-minute journey, our full carriage contained a mixture of genders and races, a microcosm of late 20th-century France. However, as the men with briefcases, and sundry other passengers, gradually left the train, the carriage became noticeably blacker and, strangely, more feminised. By the time we reached Chanteloup it was, apart from me and my husband Simon, almost entirely composed of black African women dressed in their colourful *boubous*, carrying small children and shopping bags. At that stage we had left even the suburbs behind. On the side you get off the train coming from Paris, the station stands completely isolated in a huge field, the main feature in which is a set of gigantic electric pylons. Difficult to imagine this was once the bucolic view from the writer Émile Zola's window in Médan, as described by Guy de Maupassant in *Les Dimanches d'un bourgeois de Paris* (1880). We crossed the bridge and followed the flow of passengers, towards the distinctive sight of the *cité* of Chanteloup-les-Vignes, familiar from the film. It is then that its isolation hits you.

The estate is plonked literally in the middle of a field (a map reveals the old village of Chanteloup-les-Vignes a couple of kilometres away). The planners put it there initially to house workers for a nearby Poissy car factory (see the discussion in Chapter 1 of the book). Now that the work has dried up the people of the *cité*, unless they work in Paris, are like the estate: stranded in the wilderness, the poetic name of Chanteloup-les-Vignes an ironic reminder of how bereft they are of either songs or vineyards. Quite apart from its easy access on the RER the densely mixed Villepinte, while not without its problems and mistrust between ethnic groups, seems a model of integration by comparison; my parents' immediate neighbours on the right are of Vietnamese origin (from the 1990s), and opposite lives an extended Moroccan family that has been there since the 1960s. Along the street native white French jostle with second- or third-generation *Beurs*, Jewish North Africans (*pieds noirs*), Portuguese and Eastern Europeans (blacks tend to be confined to the nearby high-rise blocks, although one family has just moved in opposite).

As we walk though the estate in Chanteloup, the impression is eerily familiar. The architecture – the curved buildings with their distinctive rooftops – is so special that we feel as if we are in the film. At first the estate is completely normal; children play and the people from the train are walking purposefully to their homes. It is about 4 p.m. on a hot Friday sunny afternoon. I take my camera out and start taking pictures of the buildings and of one or two architectural features seen in the film. Ultimately, I want to find the square where the dramatic end of the film takes place, under the mural representing Baudelaire. We find it and realise that Baudelaire and Rimbaud are two of six murals, each representing a distinguished figure from French literature (the others being Victor Hugo, Stéphane Mallarmé, Gérard de Nerval and Paul Valéry) in a circle of buildings that surround the square – a gesture typical of the laudable intention but spectacular miscalculation of this kind of urban design: why should the people of Chanteloup-les-Vignes not enjoy the symbols of great literature? And yet this gallery of 'dead white men' seems to taunt a space that appears so deprived of any other sign of culture (no cafés, restaurants or cinemas appeared to exist on the *cité*; the few shops we saw were closed; although that may have been because it was August, there was an unmistakable air of dereliction about). The square is impressive architecturally, yet the murals are almost insulting. We notice that the square is also eerily empty, except for a few youths loitering between the buildings, watching us pointing at the murals and taking pictures. At this point we hear a few clunking noises and realise it is the sound of empty cans and small rocks that are being thrown in our direction. Nothing more violent than that, but the hostility is clear. We quickly move away; they pursue us for a while and then disappear. We beat a hasty and somewhat shamefaced retreat to the station. I think of Hubert in the film saying to the television reporter: 'This is not Thoiry' (the well-known safari park). He and the young people that afternoon are right. For, while there is nothing inherently wrong in taking pictures, these youths did not mistake our intention. We had come to observe them and their habitat with our distant, learned and privileged gaze, our gesture reinforcing their deprivation. Naturally, the film had played a part in this process. We saw in Chapter 3 of this book the ambivalent attitude of the people of Chanteloup-les-Vignes, as well as other *banlieues* to *La Haine*, which has immortalised where they live as a space of violence, drug-dealing and poverty, in a gesture at once well-intentioned and narrow, insightful and patronising, turning their living space into a spectacle they only partially recognise. But the visit also threw back at me the irretrievable distance between my background as a working-class girl brought up in a working-class *cité* – and what I have become, a middle-class academic (and 'English' to boot). Generally, I like to think that I travel with ease between these spaces, and mostly I do. Back in Villepinte the ties of habits, memories and the family dynamic slot me back into my 'old' habitus. But the class gap introduces underlying tensions that occasionally resurface. The visit to Chanteloup-les-Vignes indirectly made these come to the surface, while they simultaneously brought home to me the distance between La Courneuve in the 1960s and Chanteloup-les-Vignes in the late 1990s. It also showed that Mathieu Kassovitz did not exaggerate the gulf that lies between the *cité* of *La Haine* and the Parisian city centre, 45 minutes and yet a world away.

Appendix 4: Filmographies and awards

Mathieu Kassovitz (born 1967): filmography as director

1990, *Fierrot le pou* [short]; *Peuples du monde* [music video for 'Tonton David']; 1991, *Cauchemar blanc* [short]; 1992, *Assassins* [short]; 1993, *Métisse/Café au lait*; 1995, *La Haine/Hate*; 1997, *Assassin(s)*, *Lumières sur un massacre* [short, part of anti-landmine film]; 2000, *Les Rivières pourpres/Crimson Rivers*; 2001, commercial for Le Printemps department store; *Y'a* [music video for 'Sayan Supa Crew']; 2003, *Gothika*; 2004 *Babylon Babies* [in production at time of writing]; commercials for the Sociéte Nationale des Chemins de fer Français (the French railway company)

In addition to his role as director, Mathieu Kassovitz has worked as writer or co-writer, editor, assistant director and producer on a number of his own films, as well as films by other directors.

He also has an important filmography as an actor, with leading roles notably in *Regarde les hommes tomber* (Jacques Audiard, 1993); *Métisse* (Kassovitz, 1994); *Un héros très discret* (Jacques Audiard, 1996), *Assassin(s)* (Kassovitz, 1997); *Le Fabuleux destin d'Amélie Poulain* (Jean-Pierre Jeunet, 2001) and *Amen* (Constantin Costa-Gavras, 2002).

For further details, see the internet movie database (IMDb) http://www.imdb.com/.

Awards for Mathieu Kassovitz and *La Haine*

1995 Best Direction, Cannes Film Festival
1995 Best Young Film, European Film Awards
1996 Best Editing (with Scott Stevenson), Césars
1996 Best Film, Césars
1996 Best Producer (to Christophe Rossignon), Césars

La Haine was also nominated for the 1995 Golden Palm, Cannes Film Festival and the 1995 Golden Alexander, Thessaloniki Film Festival. It also received a record eight other nominations at the 1996 Césars (Best Actor for Cassel, Best Cinematography, Best Director, Best Sound, Best Writing, Most Promising Actors for all three leads).

Awards for Mathieu Kassovitz (in addition to above)

1991 Perspectives du Cinéma Award for *Cauchemar blanc*, Cannes Film Festival

1993 Best Actor for *Métisse*, Paris Film Festival
1993 Special Jury prize for *Métisse*, Paris Film Festival
1994 Most Promising Actor for *Regarde les hommes tomber*, Césars
1995 Prix Jean Gabin ('Most promising young actor') for *Regarde les hommes tomber*
2001 Best Actor prize for *Le Fabuleux destin d'Amélie Poulain*, Cabourg Romantic Film Festival

Mathieu Kassovitz was also nominated for

1994 Best First Work for *Métisse*, Césars
1994 Most Promising Actor for *Métisse*, Césars
1997 Golden Palm for *Assassin(s)*, Cannes Film Festival
2000 Golden Seashell for *Les Rivières pourpres*, San Sebastián Film Festival
2001 Best Director for *Les Rivières pourpres*, Césars
2003 Best Actor for *Amen*, Césars

Appendix 5: A *verlan* glossary

These are the main words that I could detect in the soundtrack of the film; the spelling in some cases is my own.

Atéco: à côté = next to
Béflan: flamber = to burn, to kill
Beur: Arabe = Arab
Caillera: racaille = hoodlums, scum
Cepla: place = place
Demer: merde = shit
Gadgé: dégage = get out of here
Goleri: rigoler = to laugh
Guélar: larguer = to drop
Keuf: flic = cop
Keum: mec = bloke
Méfil: filmer = to film
Meuf: femme = woman
Oinj: joint = joint
Ouf: fou = mad
Pécho: choper = to catch
Péta: taper = to hit, strike
Rebeu: beur: arabe = arab
Relou: lourd = heavy, a drag
Renoi: noir = black
Reus: soeur = sister
S'nerev: s'énerver = to get annoyed
S'peta/s'taper = to hit each other
Tébu: buté = stubborn
Techi or teush = shit = drugs
Téci: cité = housing estate
Téma: mater = to look
Turvoi: voiture = car
Vétrou: trouver = to find
Zarbi: bizarre = strange

Appendix 6: Select bibliography

In this bibliography are indicated the main books and articles (in English and in French) on the film or its contexts. Reviews and other journalistic pieces are mentioned here if they are substantially about the film. Otherwise, references can be found in the footnotes. Similarly, books on French cinema are mentioned here only if they contain substantial sections on the film.

Aitsiselmi, Farid (ed.), *Black, Blanc, Beur: Youth Language and Identity in France*, Interface: Bradford Study in Language, Culture and Society, 5. Bradford, Bradford University Press, 2000.

Alexander, Karen, '*La Haine*', *Vertigo*, Autumn/Winter 1995.

Amiel, Vincent, 'Une nouvelle génération', *Esprit*, December 1997.

Augé, Marc, *Non-Places: Introduction to an Anthropology of Supermodernity* (translated J. Howe). London, Verso, 1995.

Beugnet, Martine, *Marginalité, sexualité, contrôle dans le cinéma français contemporain*. Paris, L'Harmattan, 2000.

Bosséno, Christian, 'Immigrant cinema: national cinema – the case of *beur* film', in R. Dyer and G. Vincendeau (eds), *Popular European Cinema*. London, Routledge, 1992.

Bourdieu, Pierre, (ed.), *La Misère du monde*. Paris, Éditions du Seuil, 1993.

Les Cahiers de la cinémathèque, special issue on the *banlieue*, 59/60, 1994.

Cannon, Steve 'Paname City rapping: B-boys in the *banlieues* and beyond', in A. Hargreaves and M. McKinney (eds), *Post-Colonial Cultures in France*. London and New York, Routledge, 1997.

Ciment, Michel and Herpe, Noël (eds), *Projections 9: French Film-makers on Film-making, in association with Positif*. London and New York, Faber and Faber, 1999.

Condé, Michel, (ed.) *La Haine, un film de Mathieu Kassovitz*. Liège, Le Centre Culturel des Grignoux et le centre de documentation du CTL., 1996.

Daeninckx, Didier, *Zapping*. Paris, Denoël Folio, 1992.

Darke, Chris, '*La Haine*', *Sight and Sound*, November 1995; also in C. Darke, *Light Readings, Film Criticism and Screen Arts*. London, Wallflower, 2000.

Dubet, François, *La galère: jeunes en survie*. Paris, Fayard, 1987.

Durand, Alain-Philippe (ed.), *Black, Blanc, Beur: rap music and hip-hop culture in the Francophone world*. Lanham; MD, Scarecrow Press, 2002.

Favier, Gilles and Kassovitz, Mathieu, *Jusqu'ici tout va bien…* Arles, Actes Sud, 1995.

Fielder, Adrian, 'Poaching on public space: urban autonomous zones in the French *banlieue* films', in M. Shiel and T. Fitzmaurice (eds), *Cinema and the City: Film and Urban Societies in a Global Context*. Oxford and Malden, MA, Blackwell, 2001.

Forbes, Jill and Street, Sarah (eds), *European Cinema, An Introduction*. London, Palgrave, 2000.

Garnier, Jean-Pierre, *Des Barbares dans la cité: de la tyrannie du marché à la violence urbaine*. Paris, Flammarion, 1996.

Hargreaves, Alec G. and McKinney, Mark (eds), *Post-Colonial Cultures in France*. London and New York, Routledge, 1997.

Higbee, Will, 'Screening the "other" Paris: cinematic representations of the French urban periphery', in *La Haine* and *Ma 6-T Va Crack-er*, *Modern and Contemporary France*, 9 (2), 2001, pp. 197–208.

J.D., 'interview du fanzine *Steadycam*', available online on Mathieu Kassovitz's official website: http://www.mathieukassovitz.com/itw/steadycam.htm, copyright 1998/2004 (accessed June 2004).

Konstantarakos, Myrto, 'Which mapping of the city? *La Haine* (Kassovitz, 1995) *and the cinéma de banlieue*', in P. Powrie (ed.), *French Cinema in the 1990s: Continuity and Difference*. Oxford, Oxford University Press, 1999.

Marie, Michel, (ed.), *Le jeune cinéma français*. Paris, Nathan, 1998.

Maspéro, François, *Les Passagers du Roissy-Express*. Paris, Éditions du Seuil, 1990; translated by P. Jones as *Roissy Express*. London, Verso, 1994.

Merle, Pierre, *Argot, Verlan et Tchatches*. Toulouse, Éditions Milan, 1997.

Mongin, Olivier, 'Regarde-les tomber; à propos de *La Haine*', *Esprit*, August–September 1995.

Morrison, Susan, '*La Haine*, *Fallen Angels*, and some thoughts on Scorsese's Children', *CineAction!*, December 1995.

Naficy, Hamid, *An Accented Cinema: Exilic and Diasporic Filmmaking*. Princeton, NJ, Princeton University Press, 2001.

Prédal, René, *Le Jeune Cinéma français*. Paris, Nathan, 2002.

Reader, Keith, 'After the riot', *Sight and Sound*, November 1995.

Reynaud, Bérénice, 'Le 'hood', *Film Comment*, 32 (2), 1996.

Robache, Thomas and Saragoussi, Pierre, *Banlieues: tant que ça tiendra*. Paris, Denoël, Documents Actualités, 1998.

Romney, Jonathan, *Short Orders: Film Writing*. London, Serpent's Tail, 1997.

Rosello, Mireille, *Declining the Stereotype*. Hanover, NH and London, University Press of New England, 1998.

Stafford, Roy, York Film Notes. *La Haine* (*Hate*). London, York Press, 2001.

Styan, David, 'So far … everything is OK!', *Vertigo*, Autumn/Winter 1995.

Tarr, Carrie, 'Ethnicity and identity in *Métisse* and *La Haine* by Mathieu Kassovitz', in T. Chafer (ed.), *Multicultural France*, Working Paper on Contemporary France no. 7, University of Portsmouth, 1997.

Tarr, Carrie, 'Ethnicity and identity in the *cinéma de banlieue*', in P. Powrie (ed.), *French Cinema in the 1990s: Continuity and Difference*. Oxford, Oxford University Press, 1999.

Trémois, Claude-Marie, *Les Enfants de la liberté: le jeune cinéma français des années 90*. Paris, Éditions du Seuil, 1995.

Vincendeau, Ginette, 'Designs on the *banlieue*: Mathieu Kassovitz's *La Haine* (1995)', in S. Hayward and G. Vincendeau (eds), *French Film: Texts and Contexts* (2nd ed.). London and New York, Routledge, 2000.